LOG
Ready for takeoff!
EST. 1ST CENTURY
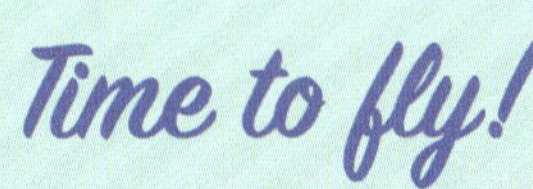
Time to fly!

PAL
PROPHECY AIRLINES

SKIES.
EST. 1ST CENTURY

BOARDING PASS FLIGHT 1910
FLIGHT 1910

PAL
PROPHECY AIRLINES
PROPHECY PROS
NAME
DATE
DEPARTURE
DESTINATION
FLIGHT 1910
PAL

PAL
PROPHECY AIRLINES

MODEL
777 PILOT RECORDS
PAL
PROPHECY AIRLINES
OFFICIAL
FLIGHT
LOG
Ready for takeoff!
EST. 1ST CENTURY

PAL
PROPHECY AIRLINES

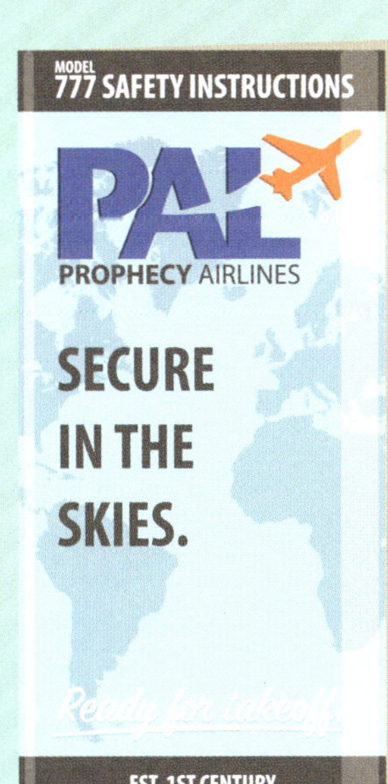
MODEL
777 SAFETY INSTRUCTIONS
PAL
PROPHECY AIRLINES
SECURE
IN THE
SKIES.
EST. 1ST CENTURY
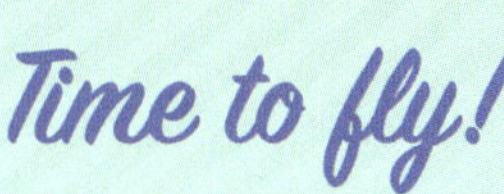
Time to fly!

PAL
PROPHECY AIRLINES

FLIGHT 1910

NAME
DATE
DEPARTURE
FLIGHT 1910
PAL

PAL
PROPHECY AIRLINES

BOARDING PASS FLIGHT 1910
FLIGHT 1910

PROPHECY PROS

PAL
PROPHECY AIRLINES

NAME
DATE
DEPARTURE
FLIGHT 1910
PAL

PAL
PROPHECY AIRLINES
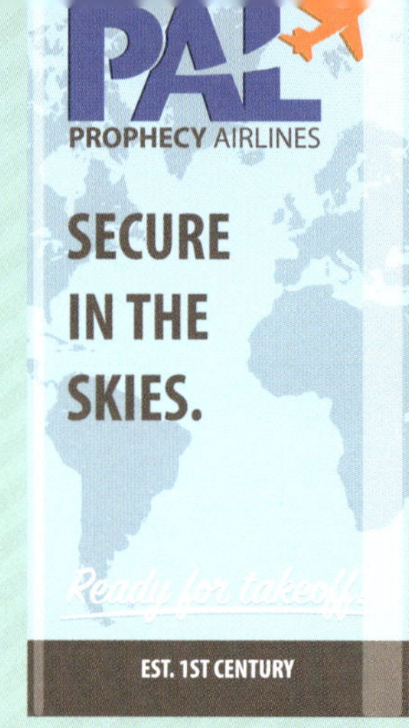
PAL
PROPHECY AIRLINES
SECURE
IN THE
SKIES.
Ready for takeoff!
EST. 1ST CENTURY

LOG
Ready for takeoff!
EST. 1ST CENTURY
Time to fly!

G PASS FLIGHT 1910
FLIGHT 1910
PAL
PROPHECY AIRLINES
Ready for takeoff!
NAME
DATE
DEPARTURE
DESTINATION
FLIGHT 1910
PAL
PROPHECY AIRLINES

PAL
PROPHECY AIRLINES

BOARDING PASS FLIGHT
PROPHECY PROS
PAL
PROPHECY AIRLINES
Ready for takeoff!

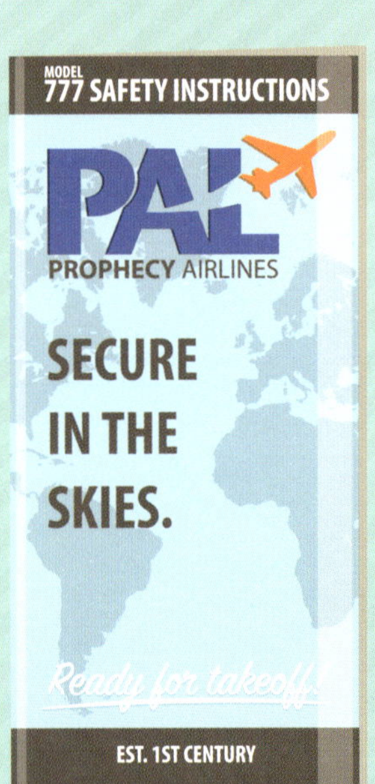
MODEL
777 SAFETY INSTRUCTIONS
PAL
PROPHECY AIRLINES
SECURE
IN THE
SKIES.
Ready for takeoff!
EST. 1ST CENTURY

MODEL
777 PILOT RECORDS
PAL
PROPHECY AIRLINES
OFFICIAL
FLIGHT
LOG
Ready for takeoff!
EST. 1ST CENTURY
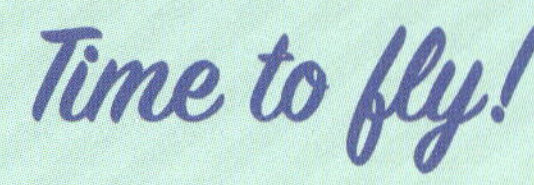
Time to fly!
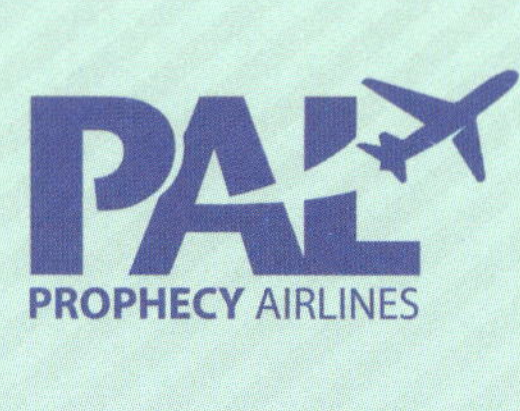
PAL
PROPHECY AIRLINES

PAL
PROPHECY AIRLINES
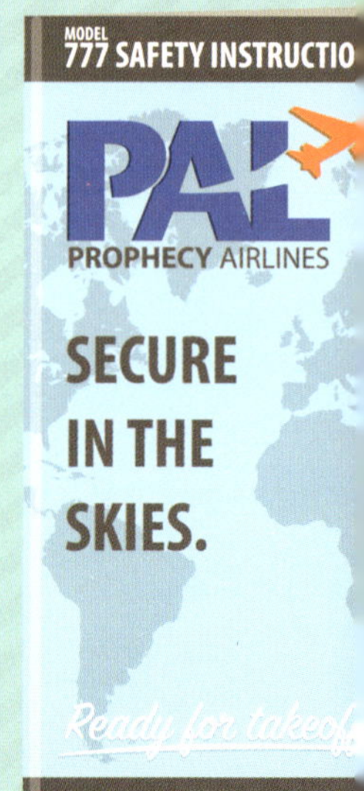
MODEL
777 SAFETY INSTRUCTIO
PAL
PROPHECY AIRLINES
SECURE
IN THE
SKIES.
EST. 1ST CENTURY

PAL
PROPHECY AIRLINES

BOARDING PASS
PROPHECY PROS

FLIGHT 1910
PAL
PROPHECY AIRLINES
Ready for takeoff!

FLIGHT 1910
NAME
DATE
DEPARTURE
FLIGHT 1910
PAL

PAL
PROPHECY AIRLINES

"The importance of prophecy should be evident, even superficially, in examining the Christian faith, for about one-fourth of the Bible was prophecy when it was written. It is evident that God intended to draw aside the veil of the future and to give some indication of what His plans and purposes were for the human race and the universe as a whole...

"The revelation of prophecy in Scripture serves as an important evidence that the Scriptures are accurate in their interpretation of the future. Because approximately half of the prophecies of the Bible have already been fulfilled in a literal way, it gives a proper intellectual basis for assuming that prophecy yet to be fulfilled will likewise have a literal fulfillment. At the same time it justifies the conclusion that the Bible is inspired of the Holy Spirit and that prophecy, which goes far beyond any scheme of man, is instead a revelation by God of that which is certain to come to pass."

John F. Walvoord, *The Prophecy Knowledge Handbook*, page 10

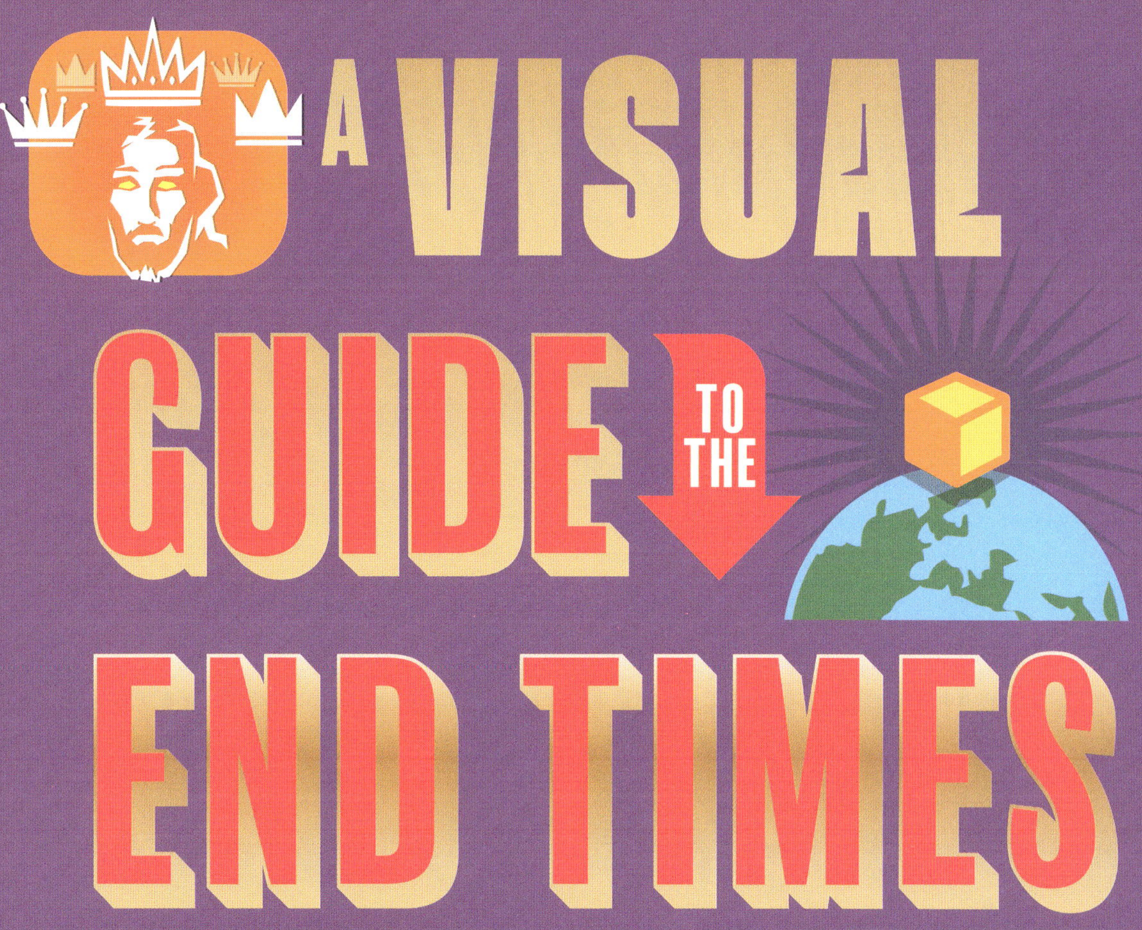

A VISUAL GUIDE TO THE END TIMES

JEFF KINLEY AND TODD HAMPSON

HOSTS OF THE *PROPHECY PROS PODCAST*

HARVEST PROPHECY

AN IMPRINT OF HARVEST HOUSE PUBLISHERS

Published in association with William K. Jensen Literary Agency, 119 Bampton Court, Eugene, Oregon 97404.

Cover design by Kyler Dougherty
Cover illustrations © Todd Hampson
Interior design by Janelle Coury

For bulk, special sales, or ministry purchases, please call 1-800-547-8979. Email: CustomerService@hhpbooks.com.

A VISUAL GUIDE TO THE END TIMES

Published by Harvest House Publishers
Eugene, Oregon 97408
www.harvesthousepublishers.com

ISBN 978-0-7369-8945-9 (hardcover)

Library of Congress Control Number: 2024951553

Printed in China

26 27 28 29 30 31 32 33 / RDS / 10 9 8 7 6 5 4 3 2

We dedicate this book to the precious bride of Christ and to "remnant believers" who long for biblical discernment in these last days.

"For the testimony of Jesus is the spirit of prophecy."

Revelation 19:10

MODEL
777 SAFETY INSTRUCTIONS

PAL
PROPHECY AIRLINES

SECURE
IN THE
SKIES.

Ready for takeoff!

EST. 1ST CENTURY

ACKNOWLEDGMENTS

A special thanks to Steve, Becky, and Nate Miller along with the rest of the incredible team at Harvest House Publishers for their vision, flexibility, editing expertise, theological acumen, and tireless efforts in helping make this book concept a reality.

CONTENTS

PART 1 Flight Plan: The Starting Point

PART 2 Cruising Altitude: The Big Events of the Last Days in Chronological Order

PART 3 Flight Crew and Passengers: Key Figures of the Last Days

PART 4 Forces of Flight: Angels and Demons of the Last Days

PART 5 Choosing Your Flight Path: Responses to Prophecy and Eschatology

PART 6 Pilot Training: Practical Tips for Leaders

PART 1

FLIGHT PLAN:
THE STARTING POINT

Are you ready to fly? To feel your feet leave the ground? To elevate your thoughts? To broaden your perspective? To deepen your faith?

To fall more in love with your Savior?

If so, then you've started reading the right book. This visual guide to the end times will give you a first-class seat toward a destination designed by God Himself in His Word. Studying Bible prophecy is an encounter in eschatology, or the study of the end times. It's like a long journey, sometimes challenging, and not without its dangers. We've chosen to portray this journey like taking a flight on an airplane. And like any flight, there is preparation, a flight plan, a time to board, a relay of safety instructions, a notification to buckle up, a time for takeoff, the enjoyment of the flight itself, and finally, landing at your destination. This book is both your boarding pass and your in-flight guide. We encourage you to take advantage of every section, and to fully enjoy the journey. And when you turn the last page of this book, our prayer is that you will indeed be blessed (Revelation 1:3) and, most importantly, more closely fellowship with the One who both scripts and supervises the future (Revelation 19:10).

Jeff Kinley

Todd Hampson

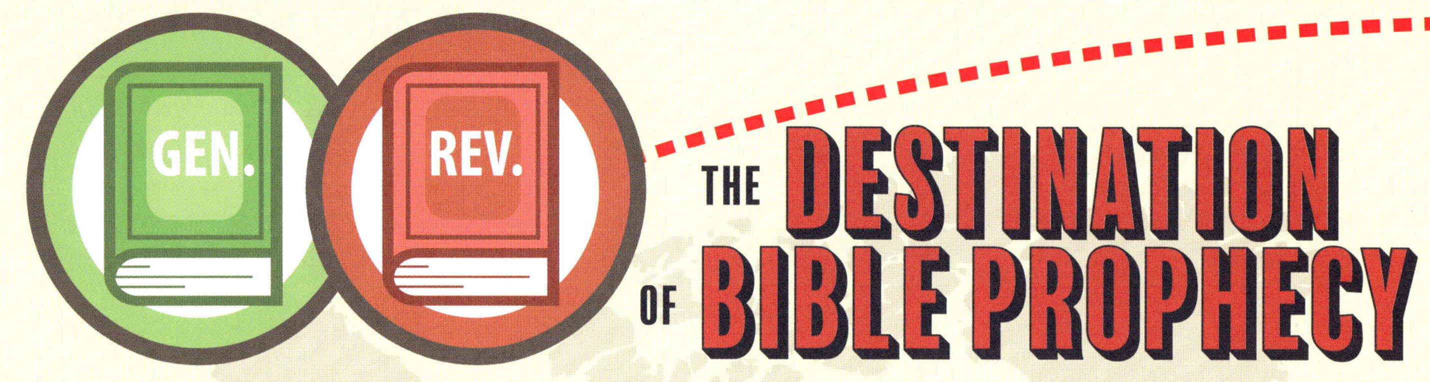

THE DESTINATION OF BIBLE PROPHECY

It has correctly been said of God that history is "His story." And why not? For if there is a God, and He is indeed the God of the Bible, then Scripture is not only true and reliable, but necessary for life itself. Only in the Bible do we find the record of the beginning of creation, the universe, the earth, and humanity. And only in Scripture do we discover how things will end and how history itself will come to a close.

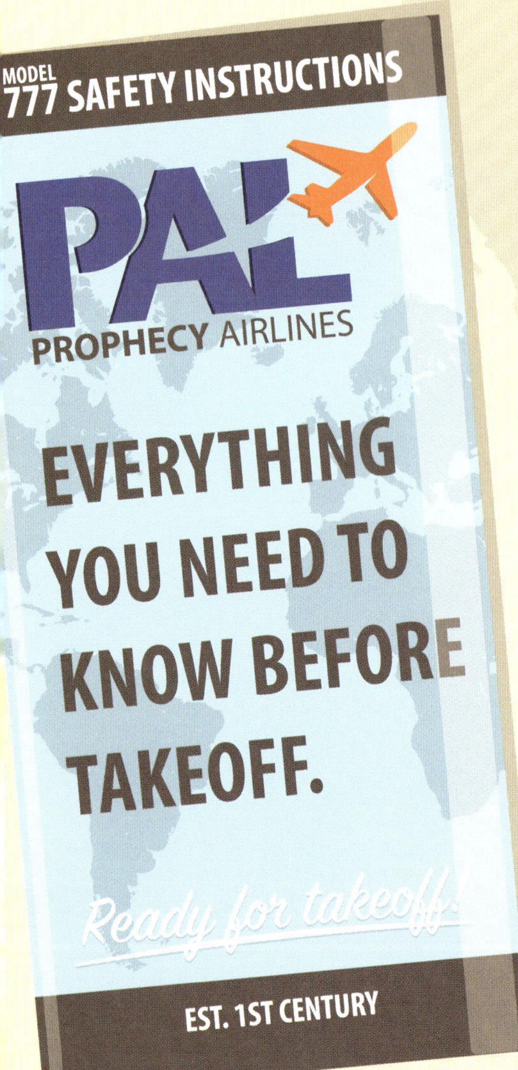

Fortunately for us, our God is a God of prophecy. What is impossible for humans to know, God graciously reveals. The prophet Daniel put it this way, "There is a God in heaven who reveals mysteries" (Daniel 2:28).

One of those mysteries is revealed early on in the very first book of the Bible. Devastated by their disobedience and the fall that infected the human race with sin, Adam and Eve were cursed by God, but not before the slithering serpent that started the whole debacle. He too received a pronouncement of judgment. Embedded within this sentence was bad news for him, but good news for mankind:

> I will put enmity between you and the woman, and between your seed and her seed; he shall bruise you on the head, and you shall bruise him on the heel (Genesis 3:15).

FROM GENESIS TO REVELATION—JESUS CHRIST

This prophecy—that foreshadowed the victory over sin, Satan, and death that Christ would win at the cross and ratify at the empty tomb—is known to theologians as the *protoevangelion*, or the first preaching of the gospel. The apostle John wrote that "the son of God appeared for this purpose, to destroy the works of the devil" (1 John 3:8).

This inaugural prophecy would be followed by hundreds of others throughout the Old Testament. In fact, every Old Testament book contains specific prophecies, with the exception of the Song of Solomon. Many of these prophecies had to do with the land of Israel, Jesus—His first and second comings, and the people of Israel—her blessings, sins, captivities, scattering, rebirth, and redemption, along with a future kingdom prepared for her. These prophecies also contain revelation about the surrounding nations, both then and in the end times.

In the New Testament, the Gospels contain the record of fulfilled prophecies regarding the Messiah, including His birth, ministry, death, resurrection, and ascension. The Epistles of Paul, Peter, and John give us a glimpse into the future, meticulously outlining Jesus' return for His bride at the rapture, the tribulation, and the defeat of the Antichrist. And yet, even though God could have ended His written Word any way He chose to, it pleased Him to inspire a book that contains up to 95 percent prophetic material.

In that last book of the Bible, we discover intricate details regarding the end times, the second coming, the judgments, the millennial kingdom, the new heavens and the new earth, and the eternal state. As it turns out, God wants His people to know what will take place in the future, how it affects them and the rest of the world, and that He is in charge of it all.

The Bible, then, is a book of prophecy because the One who wrote it is the God of prophecy. Yes, it really is His story, written and fulfilled for His glory alone.

ATTRIBUTES OF GOD IN REVELATION

The Bible, above everything else, is a book about God. Though throughout the pages of Scripture we are provided valuable information about creation, humanity, Israel, the nations, the church, angels and devils, sin and salvation, it is God Himself who is the central character. What began from Him will end with Him; as Paul wrote, "From Him and through Him and to Him are all things. To Him be the glory forever. Amen" (Romans 11:36).

It comes as no surprise then that the last book of the Bible would conclude God's written revelation by deepening our understanding of our wonderful Lord. Though we typically view Revelation primarily as a prophetic guide to the future, as it turns out, there is an even more important theme than the apocalypse embedded within, and our first clue is found in the opening verse, "The revelation *of Jesus Christ...*" (Revelation 1:1, emphasis added).

This apocalyptic vision didn't merely come to John *from* Jesus, but rather, its contents are also *about* Jesus. In chapter 1, the risen, glorified Christ is revealed to John. In chapters 2 and 3, He stands as the reprover of His churches. In chapter 4, He is sovereign, sitting upon His heavenly throne, being worshipped by the angelic hosts and the redeemed, rewarded bride. In chapter 5, He alone is worthy to break the seal, securing the title deed to planet Earth. In chapters 6 through 18, He inaugurates the tribulation-era judgments that devastate humanity and the world. In chapter 7, He is the gracious God who ignites a mighty last-days revival, saving untold millions from every nation, tribe, people group, and language. In chapter 19, He triumphantly returns to earth, faithfully fulfilling His promise. In Revelation

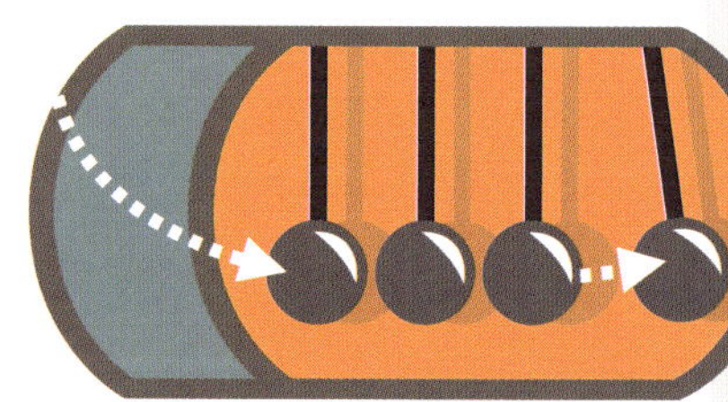

20, He reigns supremely for 1,000 years upon His throne in Jerusalem. In that same chapter, He also exercises His righteousness, judging billions of condemned unbelievers to an eternal lake of fire. In chapter 21, He recreates a new heaven and new earth, providing an eternal abode and a new Jerusalem for all the redeemed of the ages to enjoy. And in chapter 22, He lovingly issues a final invitation to all those who are presently alive to "come...Whoever desires, let him take the water of life freely" (Revelation 22:17 NKJV).

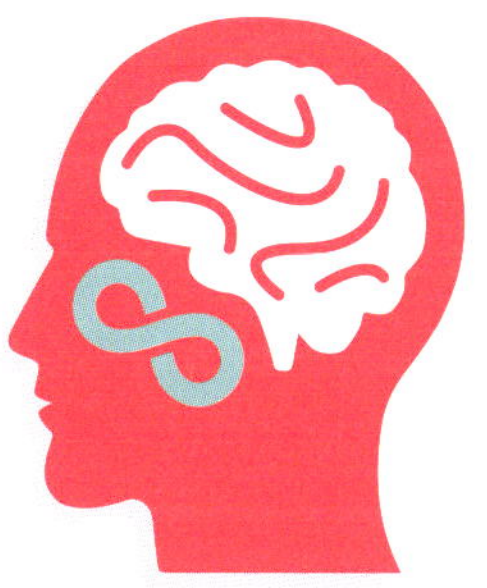

Revelation reminds us that the churches are His. The judgments we read of in Revelation belong to God and come from God. The earth's kingdoms and nations will be ruled by Him. We are reminded that Armageddon's victory is His. That all Israel will be saved by Him. That He is reprover, redeemer, rescuer, righteous judge, and the recreator and restorer of all things (Revelation 21:5).

From this we can conclude that Revelation goes far beyond information regarding the apocalypse or merely satisfying our prophetic curiosity. In fact, the book becomes one of Scripture's deepest theological studies, yielding great insights into the character and attributes of God. So if we want to engage in a solid devotional and really get to know our God, Revelation really is a good place to be.

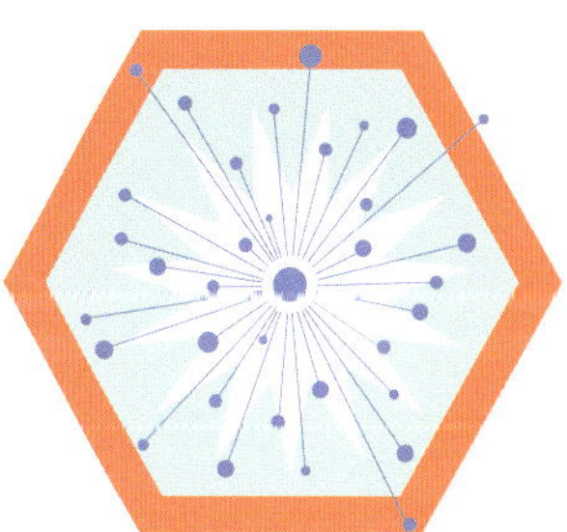

The angel who delivered Revelation's message understood this, declaring to John, "Worship God. For the testimony of Jesus is the spirit of prophecy" (Revelation 19:10).

May your study of Revelation and all of Bible prophecy (including this book) inspire you toward a greater knowledge and love of Jesus Christ!

THE IMPORTANCE OF FULFILLED PROPHECY

Anywhere from 28–30 percent of the Bible was prophetic at the time it was written. That's close to one-third of Scripture. This fact tells us that Bible prophecy is important to God, and therefore, should be to us as well. Though estimates vary depending on how one calculates past prophecies, up to 80 percent of the more than 8,000 prophetic verses found in God's Word have already been fulfilled. Not only is that an incredibly impressive track record, but it also unlocks critical intel regarding God, the Bible, humanity, and the future. Let's take a brief look at each of these, and see what we can learn.

FULFILLED PROPHECY AND GOD

The source of all prophecy, or accurately predicting future events, is God. No man, angel, or demon has the power or knowledge to forecast the future. Because God is timeless and infinite, He exists outside of the boundaries of measured time. In other words, He did not have a beginning or a moment of creation like everything else has. The psalmist put it this way, "From everlasting to everlasting, You are God" (Psalm 90:2). This is the eternality of God. But His knowledge is also infinite as well. In other words, God knows everything that is, was, will be, or could be. The Lord never learns anything. He cannot. So He has always known the future, even before it was prophetically written down by His prophets.

Further, God also possesses unlimited power to cause His prophetic revelations to come to pass. God said to Isaiah, "From eternity I am He. And there is no one who can rescue from My hand; I act, and who can reverse it?" (Isaiah 43:13 NASB). Elsewhere, Job replied to the Lord, "I know that you can do all things; no purpose of yours can be thwarted" (Job 42:2 NIV). A final truth we learn about God from fulfilled prophecy is His faithfulness. Again Isaiah records, "Truly I have spoken; truly I will bring it to pass. I have planned it, I will certainly do it" (Isaiah 46:11 NASB).

This is just one reason why Jesus, in Revelation, is called "the faithful witness" (1:5), "the faithful and true witness" (3:14 NIV), and "Faithful and True" (19:11). Jesus is the ultimate promise keeper. Therefore, fulfilled Bible prophecy tells us that God is timeless, infinite, omniscient (possessing all knowledge), omnipotent (possessing all power), and faithful. What a God!

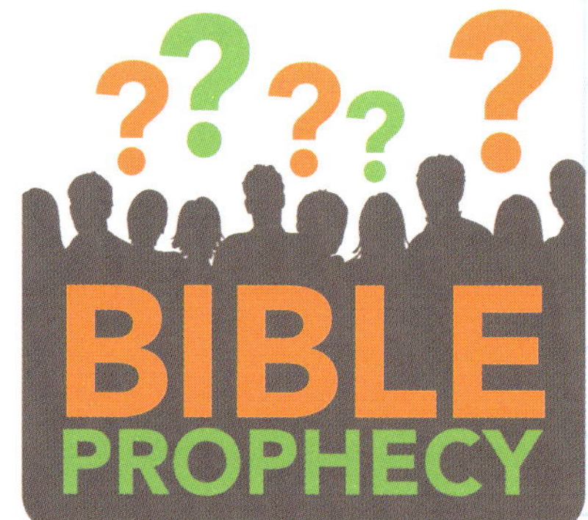

PRE-FLIGHT CHECKLIST

HOLY BIBLE

SEE INSIDE FOR 8,000 PROPHECY VERSES

FULFILLED PROPHECY AND THE BIBLE

Fulfilled prophecies show us that the Bible can be trusted. Statistically speaking, if 100 percent of all past prophecies have been fulfilled literally and precisely as prophesied, then we have every reason to believe that all future prophecies will be fulfilled in the same manner. Put another way, Scripture's pristine prophetic track record preauthenticates all remaining unfulfilled prophecies. This means that the Bible is a trustworthy and reliable source of truth. In fact, it's the only pure source of truth there is. And it also makes sense to conclude that if Scripture has always gotten it right regarding the future, then God's Word can also be trusted when it speaks to issues related to other areas, such as science, history, morality, virtue, and sexuality. In reality, the Bible has yet to be proven inaccurate in any of these areas.

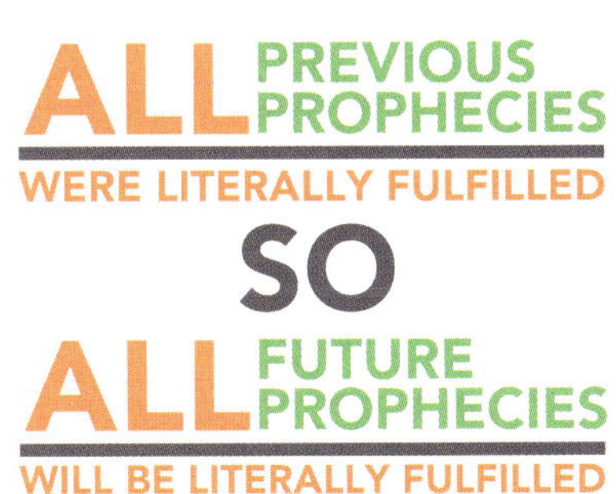

FULFILLED PROPHECY AND HUMANITY

Fulfilled prophecy reminds us that no human should be trusted regarding predictions of the future. Palm readers; fortune tellers; modern-day, so-called prophets; and all who would claim to foretell the future are automatically invalidated and disqualified due to their finite nature and limited knowledge. At best, all we can say regarding the future with any degree of confidence is what God Himself has already prophesied in His Word.

FULFILLED PROPHECY AND THE FUTURE

PROPHECY STATISTICS

28% OF THE BIBLE CONTAINS PROPHECY

1 OUT OF 30 VERSES CONTAINS PROPHECY

8,000+ TOTAL VERSES CONTAIN PROPHECY

23 OF 27 NEW TESTAMENT BOOKS MENTION THE RETURN OF CHRIST

Because of fulfilled prophecy, the future is not only known by God, but also guaranteed to take place exactly as described in Scripture. This is not to be confused with fatalism or determinism, both of which are not found in the Bible. Instead, future prophecy reflects the wise plan of an all-powerful, loving, and holy God who is bringing history toward a dramatic conclusion. God is telling a grand story, and causing it to be played out on the stage of history. And it is doubly important because we get to participate in it! This is yet another reason why pastors, churches, and individual Christians should not ignore Bible prophecy or dismiss it. Rather, we should engage it, embrace it, and experience the many benefits it brings to our lives.

WHY BIBLE PROPHECY?

There are four primary reasons why we should pay special attention to Bible prophecy in these last days:

1. Because the bride of Christ must be awake and prepared for the coming of Christ (Revelation 2–3). Jesus exhorted the church at Smyrna to "wake up" (Revelation 3:2). According to a recent study, biblical interaction is at an alarming low, with less than 10 percent of American adults engaging with the Bible one time per week, and 29 percent never reading it at all.[1] This biblical illiteracy leads to theological bankruptcy, which contributes to spiritual weakness and ineffectiveness. No wonder the church is having little impact on our culture. This theological void presents itself in our ability to discern the times and understand eschatology. Every believer is meant to read, study, and understand Bible prophecy (Revelation 1:3).

2. The church should be urgent because the era of the Antichrist approaches. Right now, we are witnessing the infrastructure for the Antichrist's one-world governance system emerge through worldwide crises, technological advances that are "shrinking" the world, the development of a global digital currency, and repeated calls from the international community to unite the nations (Daniel 2; 7; Revelation 13). As in John's day, we are now witnessing a growing spirit of antichrist (1 John 2:18; 2 Thessalonians 2:7-8). Because of this, the church's stewardship of time here is quickly coming to an end.

WHY NOW?

3 We must be urgent because the state of humanity is in rapid decline. A cloud of deception and depravity is sweeping the planet. We see it in society's blatant rejection of God and His Word and through the decline of morality, decency, and human dignity. Lawlessness in the streets, the transgender delusion, and the unashamed, ongoing mass slaughter of innocent babies each day all point to this reality (Matthew 24:37; Romans 1:18-32; Revelation 16:9, 11, 21). This deception will reach a fever pitch during the tribulation, with God Himself delivering rebellious, Christ-rejectors to a divine delusion, thus cutting off any chance of salvation (2 Thessalonians 2:10-12; Revelation 14:9-11).

4 Because the Lord's return is imminent (Romans 13:11-12; Titus 2:13; James 5:8; 1 Peter 4:7; John 14:1-3; 1 Thessalonians 4:13-18; Revelation 1:7; 19:11-16). The Bible clearly indicates that the rapture is a signless event and could occur at any time. In light of this reality, we have no time to waste. Therefore, we must be Christians who live on mission (Matthew 28:18-20), with expectancy (Philippians 3:20; Titus 2:13; James 5:8), pursuing biblical discernment (1 Peter 4:7; 1 John 2:18), displaying the light, love, and truth of Jesus (Matthew 5:14-16; Acts 1:8).

The nature of prophecy is to warn, alert, awake, and to exhibit an anticipatory spirit.

It creates alertness. Vigilance. Attention. An observant spirit. It means to be watchful. Heads up. On your toes. *Ready*.

Urgency doesn't mean to panic, fear, or even to move fast. Instead, it means to be intentional. Purposeful. And focused within the allotted time.

Brothers and sisters, let's get it done, for the time is short, and our Lord is worth it!

NOW BOARDING!

INTERPRETATION METHODS

To have a successful flight, we must make sure we are on a well-maintained plane with a working instrument panel, have a solid flight plan, and position our nose on the correct runway. These preparations are needed so that we will arrive at the proper destination—interpreting Bible prophecy accurately.

Here are the four approaches to eschatology that have been used throughout church history:

THE IDEALIST VIEW: PROPHECY IS ALLEGORY

An allegory is something that is not to be taken literally, but points to something else. The idealist school of thought arose around AD 190 from the area of Alexandria, Egypt, and was adopted by the fifth-century theologian Augustine of Hippo. This view became the official church position up to and beyond the Reformation (1517).

THE PRETERIST VIEW: THE PROPHECIES HAVE ALREADY HAPPENED

The preterist view puts forth the notion that the book of Revelation is strictly a symbolic picture of first-century events (i.e., the Roman attack on Jerusalem and the destruction of the temple in AD 70), rather than a revealing of future events that will occur at the end of the church age.

There is a spectrum of preterist positions, from partial to full-preterism, that depend on how many of these events are believed to have already taken place.

FIGURATIVE/INCONSISTENT

JUST ALLEGORY
IDEALIST

OVERVIEW OF CHURCH HISTORY
HISTORICIST

ALREADY HAPPENED
PRETERIST

LITERAL FULFILLMENT
FUTURIST
CONSISTENT HERMENEUTIC

THE HISTORICIST VIEW: PROPHECY IS MERELY AN OVERVIEW OF HISTORY

This view first appeared around AD 300 and attempts to interpret Revelation simply as a symbolic representation of the historical timeline of church history from the apostle John's time to the end. This view was popular during the Reformation era, but has many snags and versions.

THE FUTURIST VIEW: PROPHECY UNDERSTOOD LITERALLY

This view teaches that the end-time prophetic events described in Revelation are yet-future and will literally come to pass. The futurist view asserts that the hundreds of prophecies in the Bible that have already been fulfilled were fulfilled literally, not figuratively; there is no indication anywhere in Scripture that God suggests to switch to a new method of understanding prophecy; and the clear nature and pattern of Bible prophecy is: A prophecy is given, then, at a later time it is fulfilled, just as described.

TWO RUNWAYS

Using our plane analogy, there are only two runways (categories of interpretive thought) to choose from when it comes to interpreting end-times Bible prophecy—allegorical or literal.

Either Scripture can be spiritualized, with the interpreter deciding which passages have symbolic meaning, or all of Scripture is meant to be taken literally and understood by the plain and clear meanings of the words themselves.

The idealist, preterist, and historicist views all spiritualize (i.e., allegorize) Scripture in some fashion—opening the passage in question to interpretations that may stray from what the original writer intended.

The futurist view is the only approach that maintains a consistent literal understanding of Scripture from beginning to end. Just as fulfilled Bible prophecy was fulfilled literally and to the detail, so too will future prophecies about the end times and the return of Christ.

THE VARIOUS MAJOR VIEWS

The choice of runways from the previous page will impact how one views end-times prophecies. Because there is no single passage that provides every detail chronologically, in order to take flight with a logical timeline, the Bible student must consider all related prophetic details.

While what follows are not essential beliefs for salvation, logically, there can only be one correct view for each topic. Believers should study each view to see what aligns best with details of Scripture in total. Brotherly love, along with a spirit of unity and humility, should be evident when encountering others who hold a different view. We are called to be patient and gentle with one another (2 Timothy 2:24).

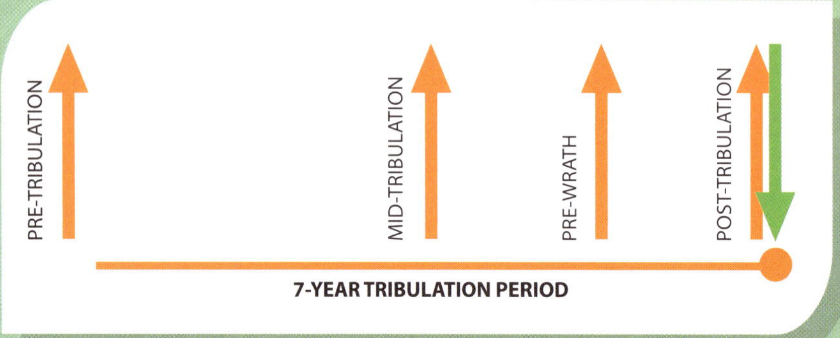

THE FOUR MOST-COMMONLY HELD VIEWS OF THE TIMING OF THE RAPTURE

The Pretribulation View This view holds that the rapture will occur prior to the start of Daniel's seventieth week (1 Thessalonians 5:9-10; Revelation 3:10), the tribulation period begins with a seven-year peace treaty brokered by the Antichrist (Daniel 9:27; 2 Thessalonians 2:3-7), and Christ will return with the armies of heaven (Zechariah 14:5; Matthew 25:31; 1 Thessalonians 3:13; 2 Thessalonians 1:7; Jude 14; Revelation 19:14) at the end of the seven-year period.

The Midtribulation View This view holds that Jesus will return at the halfway point of the seven-year tribulation. This halftime point represents the separation between the tribulation and the great tribulation. Here, Jesus' return coincides with the Antichrist's invasion of the Jewish temple and the enforcement of the mark of the beast (Revelation 12–13).

The Pre-Wrath View This view holds that the seven seal judgments will span the entire seven-year tribulation period (with the other 14 judgments scattered throughout) and asserts that God's wrath does not occur until the sixth seal—roughly five-and-a-half years into the tribulation. Believers are rescued when the sixth seal is opened (Revelation 6:12) and God's wrath begins to be poured out.

The Posttribulation View This view holds that Christians will endure all the tribulation and its horrific judgments. They will suffer and be persecuted (and some supernaturally protected), after which they will be raptured just before Christ returns at His second coming.

THE THREE MOST-COMMONLY HELD VIEWS ABOUT THE NATURE AND TIMING OF THE MILLENNIAL KINGDOM

This view holds that the millennium is not a literal 1,000-year period but is merely symbolic of the entire church age, with Christ returning at some time in the future.

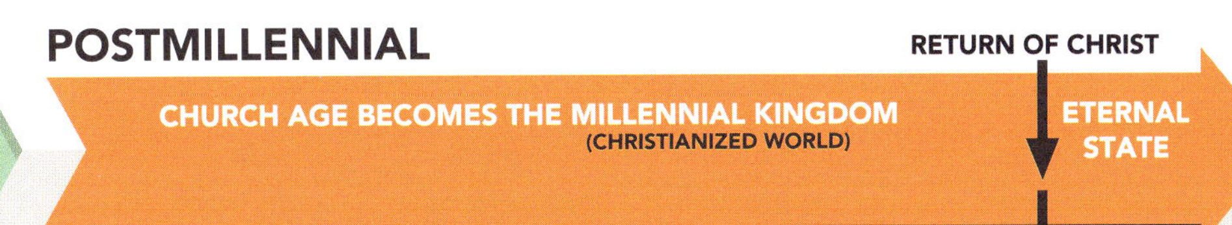

This view holds that the church will evangelize the world to such a degree that it will usher in the second coming of Christ.

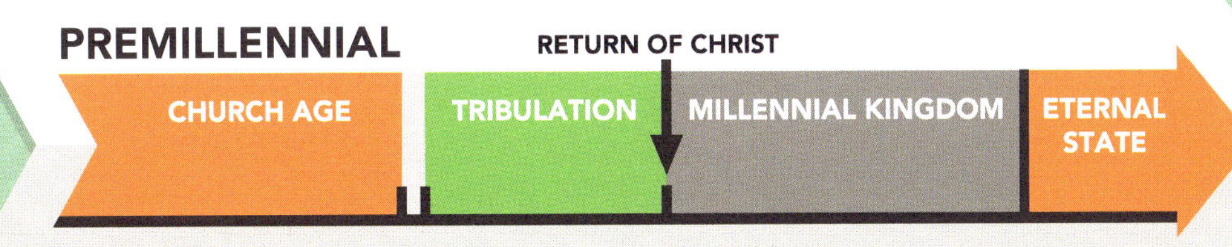

This view holds that Christ will return prior to a literal, future 1,000-year kingdom ruled by the Savior. This view sees God's unconditional promises to Abraham and David as literal, with their fulfillment in a future kingdom where Israel will enjoy the full extent of the land promised by God and Christ will reign from David's throne (Genesis 12:1; 15:18-21; 2 Samuel 7:12-16; 1 Kings 4:21).

A BRIEF HISTORY OF ESCHATOLOGY

1ST CENTURY

Ancient Pretribulationalism

During the first four centuries AD, the early church was focused on spreading the gospel and surviving intense persecution. Though not formalized in a systematic fashion, the concept of a pretribulation rapture existed and was broadly accepted in the earliest church period following the deaths of the apostles.

4TH CENTURY

Eschatology in the Dark Ages: Idealism

Around AD 190, a spiritualized view of Scripture arose from Alexandria, Egypt, and in the fourth century, it was adopted by the theologian Augustine of Hippo. Augustine applied this spiritualization to only prophetic texts, unlike the Alexandrians, who had applied it to all Scripture. Augustine's teaching became the dominant view of the Roman Catholic Church all the way into the sixteenth century. Dissenting views were considered heretical. Many people were killed for teaching doctrine that did not align with the official Roman-Catholic views. Any writings that taught other views (when found) were likewise destroyed. This interpretation method leads toward amillennialism and a figurative view of the tribulation period, but a literal return of Christ.

Eschatology of the Reformation: Historicism/Preterism

Historicism

Key figures of the Protestant Reformation, such as Martin Luther and John Calvin, did a great service to Christians everywhere by reforming many of the teachings of the established church—primarily the doctrine of salvation by grace through faith alone. Unfortunately, the reformers did not apply this return to a literal interpretation method to the events surrounding the return of Christ.

The only New Testament book for which Calvin did not write a commentary was the book of Revelation. And Luther did not use the final book of the Bible in his preaching and teaching. The reformers viewed Revelation as a symbolic overview of church history, and they applied any negative symbolism in the book to the Roman Catholic Church.

Preterism

In response, Catholic theologians developed what is known as the preterist view in an attempt to sway popular belief away from post-Reformation teaching. Preterism teaches that the events of Revelation occurred in the first century, when Rome destroyed Jerusalem in AD 70. This is still the primary eschatological view in Roman Catholicism, and has carried over to some Protestant denominations as well.

Modern Pretribulationalism Premillennialism

As more and more people gained access to the Bible in their own language, a literal understanding of prophecy returned, leading scholars to conclude that the church could look forward to literal end-times events—including a rebirth of the nation of Israel.

In 1830, John Darby systematized the literal interpretation method along with the pretribulation view of the rapture. In the 1900s, a handful of American theologians further popularized the pretribulation view in a few key seminaries, and then, it became the dominant view in America among evangelical Christians.

With the reestablishment of Israel as a nation in fulfillment of prophecy, the literal futurist approach has been thoroughly validated. This event and other current conditions that align with a literal understanding of prophecy has taken pretribulationalism premillennialism into its clearest and most developed form.

OBJECTIONS TO PRETRIBULATIONISM

Of all the promises Christians look forward to, none of them is so precious as the rapture of the church. In fact, Paul calls it our "blessed hope" (Titus 2:13). Throughout the New Testament, the early church is exhorted to eagerly anticipate this glorious event that signals the end of our struggle with sin, the perfection of our spirits, the beginning of our wedding celebration, and our rescue from God's tribulation wrath.

Today, however, no doctrine is under greater attack than is the rapture, both from atheist secularists and pastors and theologians within Christendom. In particular, this animosity and ridicule is targeted toward the pretribulation rapture, or the belief that Christ returns for His church prior to the unleashing of God's anger and wrath during the coming seven-year tribulation. But why? Here are four of the most common objections to the pretribulation rapture and responses.

OBJECTION #1

The Word Rapture Is Not Found in the Bible

RESPONSE: *True.*

This English word is not found in Scripture. However, there are also other English words that aren't found in Scripture, such as *Trinity*, *inerrancy*, *incarnation*, *Christmas*, *Great Commission*, *missions*, and *Bible*. These are all terms coined to help describe truths and doctrines that are indeed found in the Bible. So just because the English word is not in the English translation does not mean that the teaching is not.

OBJECTION #2

The Rapture Is a Recent Doctrine

RESPONSE: *Not true.*

Some erroneously claim that the rapture was invented and popularized in the nineteenth century by English Protestant theologian John Nelson Darby. However, upon careful study, one will discover that belief in a pretribulational deliverance can be found in the writings of the church fathers as early as the second century AD, and even in the first century AD in a document called the *Didache* (or *Teaching of the Twelve Apostles*, c. AD 65–80). There is also strong evidence to suggest that Irenaeus (c. AD 130–202) also held to an imminent return of Christ. Why would this be significant? Because Irenaeus was a disciple of Polycarp, who was a disciple of John (yes, *that* John). It is highly unlikely that Irenaeus would hold to a view contrary to that which John believed.

But regardless of when the doctrine of the rapture became popularized or accepted in the church, always the most important question to ask is: "What does the Bible say?" To argue the legitimacy of a particular doctrine based upon when it became popular in church history is to argue against many core doctrines of the faith, including justification by faith, which did not gain a resurgence until the Reformation (1517).

OBJECTION #3

The Rapture Is a Convenient "Escape Clause"

RESPONSE: ***As was the ark for Noah. Also, the two angels who evacuated Lot out of Sodom and Gomorrah.***

We would agree that Christians are never promised immunity from hard times or persecution (John 15:18-20; 16:33). However, we make a strong distinction between man's wrath and God's wrath. In fact, Christians are promised exemption from God's wrath because of Christ's payment for our sin at the cross (John 19:30; Romans 8:1; 2 Corinthians 5:21; 1 Thessalonians 1:10; 5:9; Revelation 3:10). There is a world of difference between tribulation and *the* tribulation.

OBJECTION #4

The Rapture Produces Lazy, Unproductive Christians

RESPONSE: ***Not necessarily; but other rapture views could.***

Other views regarding the timing of the rapture—midtribulationism, pre-wrath, and posttribulationism—all have "timestamps" attached to them. Conceivably, one could calculate the timing of the rapture in these views, and simply get themselves ready just prior to it. But the pretribulation rapture is the only view that truly embraces the doctrine of imminence, or the belief that Christ could return at any time. Other views essentially handcuff Jesus and tell Him that He cannot come back at any time. The imminent return of the Lord should be a strong motivator to always be ready for His rapture return.

KEY REASONS FOR THE PRETRIBULATION RAPTURE

There are many strong arguments for the pretribulation rapture. Here are four of them:

1 THE PATTERN OF GOD'S DELIVERANCE

God's established protocol in Scripture is to deliver the righteous prior to unleashing His apocalyptic wrath upon humanity. Examples include Enoch, Noah, and Lot, all men who were portrayed as righteous in their days of depravity. This truth is based, not in emotional convenience or wishful thinking, but rather in theology and God's character (Romans 8:1; Revelation 3:10).

2 THE PROMISE OF JESUS

On the night before His crucifixion, Jesus gathered His disciples into an upper room where He introduced for the first time the concept of the rapture. Mirroring the Jewish betrothal and marriage custom, He promised His men that following His departure to the Father's house, He would one day return and "receive you to Myself, that where I am, there you may be also" (John 14:3). Jesus is in heaven right now with the Father, preparing a place for us. And one day, perhaps soon, He will arrive unexpectedly and unannounced (just like the Jewish bridegroom) to snatch away His bride and take her to the Father's house where the wedding celebration will begin.

3 THE PROPHECY OF PAUL

First Thessalonians 4:13-18, which we will look at in more depth later, outlines the rapture in great detail. However, this wasn't the only place where the apostle Paul wrote about this glorious event. In at least 20 different New Testament passages, Paul, along with James, the author of Hebrews, Peter, Jude, and Jesus, remind believers of the rapture's reality and what our response to it should be.

4 THE PORTRAYAL OF THE CHURCH IN REVELATION

The word *church* occurs 20 times in Revelation. The breakdown is as follows:

- Chapters 1–3 = 19 times
- Chapters 6–18 = 0 times (These are the chapters covering the tribulation.)
- Chapter 22 = 1 time

By contrast, chapter 4 shows the church—represented by the 24 elders—in heaven, falling down and worshipping before Jesus, casting their bema crowns at His feet.

And, in Revelation 19, we see the bride returning *with* Jesus *from* heaven (where she has been for seven years, receiving her rewards and celebrating her marriage to the Lamb [Revelation 19:7-8, 14]). It stands to reason that to return to earth with Christ, we must have been with Him in heaven prior to His second coming. Therefore, we must have been raptured sometime before that point (i.e., before the tribulation wrath began in Revelation 6:1).

These are four strong arguments for a pretribulation rapture. There are many others, but again, we urge every believer to study the Scriptures for themselves and come to their own conclusion.

New Testament Passages that Speak of Jesus' Imminent Rapture Return

(emphasis added)

Romans 13:11	"Knowing the **time**, that it is **already** the hour."
Romans 13:12	"The night is almost gone, and the day is **near**."
1 Corinthians 1:7	"**Awaiting eagerly** the revelation of our Lord Jesus Christ."
1 Corinthians 16:22	"**Maranatha**" (used by the early church for "hello" or "goodbye," from an Aramaic expression meaning, "our Lord, come").
Philippians 3:20	"Our citizenship is in heaven, from which also we **eagerly** wait for a Savior."
Philippians 4:5	"The Lord is **near**."
1 Thessalonians 1:10	"To **wait** for His Son from heaven."
Titus 2:13	"**Looking for the blessed hope** and the **appearing** of the glory of our great God and Savior, Christ Jesus."
James 5:7-8	"Therefore be patient, brethren, until the **coming of the Lord**...be patient; strengthen your hearts, for the coming of the Lord is **near**."
Hebrews 9:28	"Christ also...will **appear a second time** for salvation without reference to sin, **to those who eagerly await Him**."
Hebrews 10:25	"Encouraging one another; and all the more **as you see the day drawing near**."
Hebrews 10:37	"For yet **in a very little while**, He who is coming **will come**, and will **not delay**."
1 Peter 1:13	"**Fix your hope** completely on the grace to be brought to you at the revelation of Jesus Christ."
1 Peter 4:7	"The end of all things is **near**."
1 John 2:18	"We **know** that it is the **last hour**."
Jude 21	"**Waiting anxiously** for the mercy of our Lord Jesus Christ."
Revelation 3:11	"**I am coming quickly**; hold fast what you have."
Revelation 22:7	"Behold, **I am coming quickly**."
Revelation 22:12	"Behold, **I am coming quickly**."
Revelation 22:20	"Yes, **I am coming quickly**."

SYMBOLS

There are symbols in the Bible and in Bible prophecy, where we see riders on horses, beasts, serpents, bowls, horns, stars, and many others. However, all these word pictures point to literal truths. Always. A *symbol* is a word or phrase that represents something other than itself. And Revelation, for example, is full of symbols that are explained in either the immediate context, some other place in the book, or in the broader context of Scripture (particularly the Old Testament prophets).

There are seven basic categories of symbols that show up in Revelation: animals, colors, earthly objects, celestial objects, man-made objects, people, and numbers. We read about symbols such as the seven lamp stands, the beast that rises out of the sea, a beast with seven heads and ten horns, a woman riding a beast, the seven seals, the seven scrolls, the seven bowls, the "four horsemen of the Apocalypse," and the Lamb seen in heaven's throne room. As you study Revelation, you can have confidence that the symbols have a specific discernible meaning. Once a symbol is understood, it brings fresh meaning to the text and practical insight into how these symbols relate to end-times events.

FIGURES OF SPEECH

Sometimes we find poetic language and other clear figures of speech in Scripture. It's obvious they should not be interpreted literally. For example, Jesus frequently used hyperbole in His parables as He talked about things like camels fitting through the eye of a needle, or pointing out a speck of dirt in someone else's eye while we have a plank in our own eye.

Many other figures of speech are used in Scripture including simile, metaphor, irony, personification, metonymy, hendiadys, and synecdoche, to name a few. The Bible is a linguistic masterpiece, and the figures of speech serve to heighten the meaning, not to confuse it. As with symbols, where figures of speech are used, readers can understand the plain meaning by the context of the passage, by the historical background, and by the original audience. There is no reason to attempt to allegorize the text to mean anything other than its plain sense meaning.

TWO MAIN SYSTEMS: **DISPENSATIONALISM**

DISPENSATIONALISM

Dispensationalism is a theological system that teaches the Bible should be consistently interpreted literally from Genesis to Revelation, leading to the conclusion that God has used different dispensations (or divine administrations—Greek word *oikonomia*, meaning economy, stewardship, or administration) in history to bring about His redemptive plan. The word *oikonomia* is used nine times in the New Testament.

Also, this literal interpretation leads to the conclusion that God has two distinct programs—one for Israel and one for the church—and that He has worked progressively in different time periods of biblical history. This view acknowledges the clear fact that the church is no longer under the law of the Mosaic covenant and that salvation comes through faith in Jesus Christ alone. But it also acknowledges the unconditional promises related to the Abrahamic and Davidic covenants and awaits the literal fulfillment of future prophecies related to Israel and the Jewish people. It views the modern rebirth of Israel as literal fulfilled prophecy.

Classical dispensationalism teaches seven dispensations; however, the real distinctives of this theological system is not the number of dispensations but the literal interpretation method it uses from Genesis 1:1 to Revelation 22:21, the view that prophecy will be literally fulfilled, and that God is not done with His unconditional promises to the Jewish people.

DISPENSATIONAL FORCES OF FLIGHT

DISTINCT DISPENSATIONS

LIFT

DISTINCTION BETWEEN ISRAEL & THE CHURCH

DRAG

THRUST

LITERAL HERMENEUTIC

WEIGHT

PRETRIB/PRE-MIL

DISPENSATIONS

CREATION
INNOCENCE
FALL
CONSCIENCE
FLOOD
HUMAN GOVT.
ABRAHAM
PROMISE
LAW
LAW
1ST COMING
GRACE
2ND COMING
KINGDOM
FINAL JUDGMENT

AND COVENANT THEOLOGY

COVENANT THEOLOGY

Covenant theology is a framework for understanding the story of the Bible through the lens of (primarily) two overarching covenants in Scripture—the covenant of works and the covenant of grace. It views the church as, in essence, having been in existence since God first established a covenant of grace with Adam.

It sees the Jewish people as being a starting point, so to speak, that would grow to include elect believers from all nations. In essence, it views the church as an expansion, offshoot, or continuation of Israel. Many covenant theologians hold to a view known as replacement theology (also known as supersessionism), which teaches that the church has replaced Israel and that all promises to Israel have now been conferred onto the church.

Covenant theology does not use a literal interpretation method when it comes to eschatology or the prophecies related to Israel and the Jewish people. It views most of Revelation as allegory and does not view the modern rebirth of Israel (or anything related to the Jewish people) as a fulfillment of prophecy.

Dispensationalism and Covenant Theology have many differences, and lead to vastly different conclusions about important doctrines, but both align with orthodox beliefs when it comes to the essentials of Christianity. Most notably, both systems teach that salvation is by grace alone, through faith alone in Christ alone.

THE PROPHETIC DISTINCTIONS

One of the biggest mistakes people make in Bible interpretation is to assume that the church has replaced Israel as God's "chosen people." It is true that all believers are described as being "elect" (Romans 8:33), or chosen (Ephesians 1:4; John 15:16; Titus 1:1). But we must make a distinction between individuals, the church, and the nation of Israel. To begin, nowhere in Scripture is the covenant relationship that God established with the nation of Israel permanently negated or nullified. Consider that God's redemptive plan for humanity began in the garden of Eden when He slew an animal (likely a lamb) and shed its blood as a foreshadowing of His ultimate provision for sin through Christ (Genesis 3:21; John 1:29). This sin-bearing Messiah would be born a Jewish baby through a Jewish lineage that began with a man named Abram (Abraham). Through him, God would birth a people, a nation with whom He would have a special covenantal relationship, and to whom He would make several binding unconditional promises.

To Abram, God promised a portion of land in addition to making a great nation out of his lineage (Genesis 12:1-2; 15:5-6). This covenant God made with Abram is unconditional, meaning God is the party responsible to fulfill the agreement, as He is the only one who signed the contract (Genesis 15:1-18). This land covenant has never been fully ratified, as Israel has never possessed all the land God promised to them (Genesis 15:18-21).

Another promise God made to Israel was a descendant of David would sit on his throne, establishing a kingdom that would last forever (2 Samuel 7; 1 Chronicles 17:11-14; 2 Chronicles 6:16). This too was an unconditional covenant, referred to as the Davidic covenant. It also has not yet been fulfilled. When Jesus inaugurated His ministry, He offered the kingdom to the Jewish people but was rejected by the Jewish religious leaders. As a result, God's discipline on Israel was that she would suffer and be in a state of disbelief, or partial hardening, until the last days (Romans 11:25). God placed national Israel on the back burner until the end times, when He will once again return His attention directly to her for her ultimate rescue and redemption (Zechariah 12:10; Romans 11:26).

BETWEEN ISRAEL AND THE CHURCH

Meanwhile, God birthed a new people (the church, the bride of Christ) that is made up of individual Jews and Gentiles (Romans 10–11; Ephesians 2:11-14). When the church age is complete and the last person is saved, God will once again turn His attention back toward the nation of Israel and the Jewish people (Romans 11:25). The miracle of Israel having become a nation again in 1948, after nearly 2,000 years of being exiled and scattered around the world, is prophetic proof that God is winding down the church age and returning once again to His covenant relationship with Israel. He is doing this because He is a covenant-keeping God, and He is incapable of breaking His promises to that tiny nation (Romans 11:29).

In summary, the prophetic promises made to Israel are:

- physical return to the land (Deuteronomy 30:3; Ezekiel 36–37). Status: fulfilled, with ongoing fulfillment.
- spiritual return to the Lord in salvation (Zechariah 12:10; Matthew 23:39; Romans 11:26). Status: unfulfilled.
- establishment of the Messianic kingdom (Isaiah 9:6-7; Revelation 20). Status: unfulfilled.

As for the church, she has been promised rescue from the coming tribulation wrath and inclusion into that Messianic kingdom (2 Timothy 2:12; Revelation 5:10). These two entities—national Israel and the church—are distinct in their nature, purpose, and role in the end times.

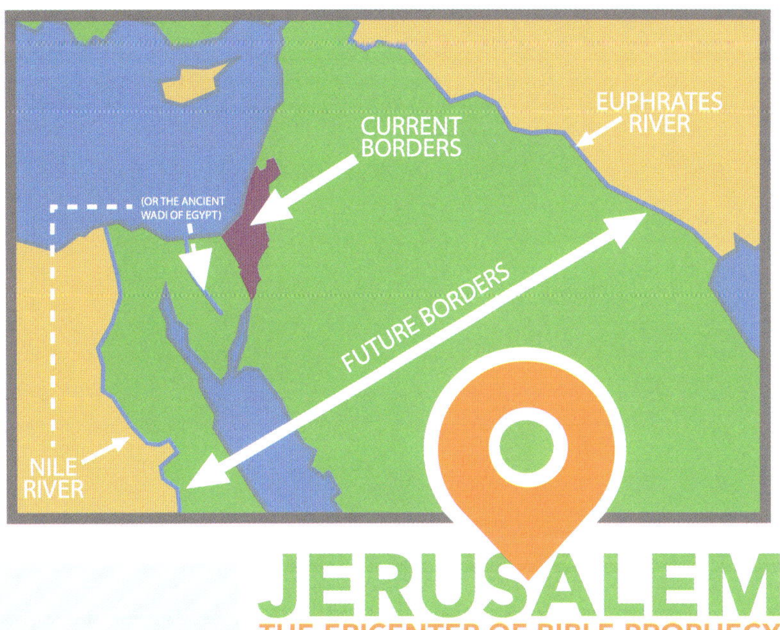

PART 2

CRUISING ALTITUDE:

THE BIG EVENTS OF THE LAST DAYS IN CHRONOLOGICAL ORDER

One of the most confusing things about Bible prophecy is trying to put the events in their proper order. This can be made difficult because of contrasting and conflicting views that Christian leaders have regarding the end times. But even apart from that, it requires time for a robust study of the Scriptures to discover the domino-like effect each event has on the next.

It is important to note that God is a God of sequence and order. And His acts are in accordance with His prophetic plan for the ages. In Genesis 1–3, Moses records for us the sequential order of the creation account. This historical narrative follows six 24-hour days, one after another, with each containing their own chronological suborder. And though our English Bible's Old Testament books are not arranged sequentially, God nevertheless tells the story of mankind, the nations, and of Israel in their individual and connecting contexts.

So when we come to the last-days prophecies, we would expect to understand them in some sort of logical order and format. Fortunately, Scripture provides us this order. And though there may be some interpretive disagreements concerning a few details and timeline specifics, we can still trace the general story here with confidence.

So where do we begin? Let's look at God's end-times narrative in chronological order as portrayed in the Bible.

THE RAPTURE

Despite the fact that some authors, pastors, and teachers claim that prophecies are being fulfilled all around us, no actual last-days prophecies have come to pass in recent history with the exception of Israel becoming a nation again in 1948. What we are currently witnessing are the precursors to those last-days prophecies recorded primarily in Daniel, the Gospels, and Revelation. We are seeing the foreshocks of those biblical predictions. Like a child being formed in the womb, we can confidently say that a baby is on the way and that the times are "prophetically pregnant."

So then, what is the next prophetic event on God's calendar? We believe it to be the rapture of the church.

Unlike most last-days prophecies, the rapture has no definite precursors or warning signs. In other words, it's a signless event. This is why we believe in what is called the doctrine of imminency, or the belief that Christ could return at any time. The early church certainly held this belief, as virtually every mention of the rapture contains some sense of imminency. As previously mentioned, the rapture is an event that involves both a rescue and a romance. The twofold purpose of this unique prophecy is to deliver the bride of Christ from the coming tribulation wrath (1 Thessalonians 1:10; 5:9; Revelation 3:10) and culminates in our wedding union to our groom, the Lord Jesus Christ (John 14:1-2; 2 Corinthians 11:2; Revelation 19:7-8).

One compelling reason why we believe the church will not endure the coming seven-year tribulation is because the purposes of that tribulation have nothing to do with the bride of Christ, but only with unbelieving humanity and the nation of Israel. At the rapture, all living believers are snatched away from planet Earth and this present evil age, and they are transported up to heaven with Christ, who has met them in the air (1 Thessalonians 4:16-17). More about the specific details of the rapture on the next page!

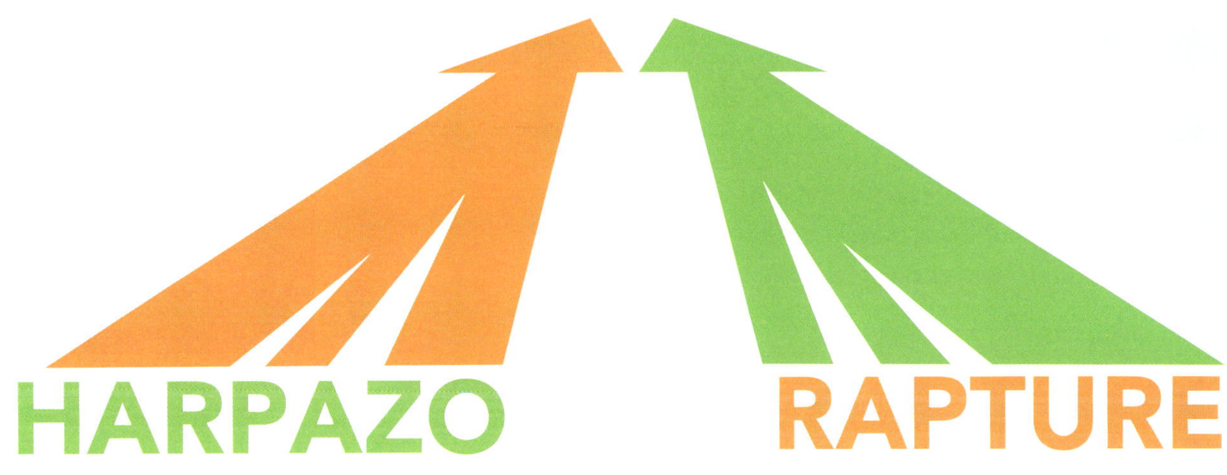

THE RAPTURE IN SLOW MOTION

1 THESSALONIANS 4

As with other areas of theology, when God speaks concerning eschatology, He is very specific and intentional. The last book God wrote contains some 95 percent prophecy and includes an enormous amount of detailed information. But why? It's because He doesn't want His children to be in the dark concerning the last days. Regarding the rapture, it's no different.

Paul begins his treatment of the rapture in 1 Thessalonians this way, "But we do not want you to be uninformed, brethren, about those who are asleep" (1 Thessalonians 4:13). He then breaks down the rapture frame by frame, in "slow motion." First, he states the certainty of the rapture based upon the historical reality of Jesus' resurrection (4:14). In other words, if one (the resurrection) occurred, then the other (the rapture) is certain to occur. That's how sure and guaranteed the rapture is!

Second, Paul's authority on this teaching is "by the word of the Lord" (4:15). In case anyone doubts the rapture, the apostle says this teaching carries the full authority and weight of, *Thus says the Lord*.

Let's break down the chronology of this amazing event. Think of it as frames in a movie reel.

FRAME 1

Jesus Christ personally returns from heaven. Remember, the Lord hasn't physically broken through earth's atmosphere in 2,000 years (cf. Acts 1:9-11). However, unlike His second coming (Zechariah 14:4), which occurs at the end of the tribulation, Jesus won't touch down on earth, but rather, stop in the atmosphere (1 Thessalonians 4:17). He will also shout something as He descends, though no one knows what He will say. Some speculate it could be similar to what He said to John when he was invited up to heaven (Revelation 4:1; see also John 5:28; 11:43).

FRAME 2

An archangel shouts (1 Thessalonians 4:16). This same Greek word for "voice" is used 55 times in Revelation, and virtually every time it refers to a loud sound or voice. There is only one archangel named in Scripture, Michael, though we know there is more than one (Daniel 10:13; 12:1; Jude 9). And what will this mighty angel shout? Again, we are not told. Perhaps something similar to, "But at midnight, there was a shout. 'Behold, the bridegroom! Come out to meet him'" (Matthew 25:6).

FRAME 3

The dead in Christ are raised (1 Thessalonians 4:16). Every Christian, from the first martyr Stephen to the last church-age believer to die, will be supernaturally resurrected from the grave. Their spirits have been with Jesus since the moment of their death (2 Corinthians 5:8). But now it's time to receive a new and glorified body. Corpses will come alive, as millions of graves are divinely and instantly dug up. All believers' bodies destroyed by fire, war, the sea, or time itself will be miraculously recreated and reformatted for heaven's atmosphere and the presence of a holy God.

FRAME 4

Living believers are raptured/snatched away (1 Thessalonians 4:17). Following Jesus' grave-busting miracle, we who are alive are transported upward. This will be an unforgettable flight. A takeoff for the ages! Immediately, we are transformed into Christlikeness, in spirit and in body (1 Corinthians 15:51-52; 1 John 3:1-3). Death and the sin nature will be eradicated from our lives forever.

FRAME 5

We begin eternity with Jesus (1 Thessalonians 4:17). Our life pursuit will finally become a reality—we get to be with our Lord. This also fulfills a 2,000-year-old promise Christ made to His disciples on the Thursday night of His betrayal and arrest (John 14:1-3). And what is the biblical response to this incredible moment of destiny? Paul concludes, "Therefore comfort one another with these words" (1 Thessalonians 4:18; cf. 5:11). So, through God's careful explanation of the rapture, we can receive confidence, clarity, expectation, assurance, anticipation, and hope!

THE BEMA SEAT

The rapture is immediately followed by the *bema*, or the judgment seat of Christ (1 Corinthians 3:10-15; 4:5; 2 Corinthians 5:10). There is much we can know about this judgment beyond simply its timing.

1 The bema is not a judgment for sins. Our sins and God's eternal forgiveness of them were forever dealt with at the moment we trusted Jesus for salvation (Romans 8:1; Colossians 1:13-14; 2:13-14). There is not even a drop of condemnation awaiting us in the next life. Jesus paid it all, and we are completely and forever forgiven through Him and His substitutionary death for our sins (Hebrews 7:23-24).

Quite the contrary, this judgment is strictly for rewards. It's an awards ceremony. The Greek word *bema* comes from ancient-Greek athletic competition. When runners completed a race in the arena, they would stand before the judge of the games, who was seated on a large, elevated stone seat called the bema. He would determine, after carefully watching the race, who had earned the prize and who would receive no prize. Typically, an olive-branch crown was awarded to the winners. But like today, these prominent athletes also enjoyed a sort of celebrity status in the community, along with other tangible benefits.

2 The bema is only for church-age believers (2 Corinthians 5:10). Only the bride will appear before Christ's throne at this particular judgment. Old Testament saints will receive their reward and their resurrection at the second coming of Christ (Daniel 12:1-3).

3 All believers will be raptured and receive an audience before Christ (1 Corinthians 4:5; 2 Corinthians 5:10). Scripture does not teach a partial rapture, or that only those believers who are living right at the time of the rapture will make it to heaven for the awards ceremony.

4 Not all Christians will be rewarded equally. Some will receive crowns and additional rewards, while others will suffer loss of reward, yet "he himself will be saved, yet so as through fire" (1 Corinthians 3:15). Other rewards include reigning with Christ in His kingdom (2 Timothy 2:12; Revelation 5:10; 20:4, 6; 22:5).

5 The bema will take place after the rapture, but before the second coming (1 Corinthians 4:5; Revelation 19:7-8). This is yet another biblical evidence of the pretribulational rapture, or that we will be in heaven while the seven-year tribulation takes place on earth.

6 Various crowns will be awarded at the bema, including:

- the imperishable crown (1 Corinthians 9:24-25)
- the crown of life (James 1:12)
- the crown of exultation (1 Thessalonians 2:18-20)
- the crown of righteousness (2 Timothy 4:8)
- the crown of glory (1 Peter 5:1-4)

7 Jesus will expose our works to His fiery judgment (1 Corinthians 3:13-15). Deeds done for Christ will be reviewed. They will all be tested to see if they are worthy of reward.

8 Our works will be judged based on our motives at the time of our service (1 Corinthians 4:5). Works done for attention, self-esteem, or personal gain will be burned up, while those done with pure motives for Jesus and His glory will remain and be praised.

9 Not a single good work—large or small, seen or unseen—will go unnoticed by the Lord. He sees everything you do for Him, and will reward you for your service (1 Corinthians 15:58).

10 We will use our crowns to heap even more praise upon Jesus (Revelation 4:10). It was Jesus who saved us, who sustained us, and who enabled us to serve Him while on earth. He deserves all our praise because He is worthy (Revelation 4:11).

The church-age saints will spend the tribulation in heaven, receiving rewards, rejoicing in their marriage to the Lamb, returning glory and praise to Him, and resting in His presence.

PEACE COVENANT

In Daniel 9:27, the prophet describes the event that will prove to be the "game changer" of the end times:

> He will make a firm covenant with the many for one week, but in the middle of the week he will put a stop to sacrifice and grain offering; and on the wing of abominations will come one who makes desolate, even until a complete destruction, one that is decreed, is poured out on the one who makes desolate.

From the context of this passage, the "many" here refers to the people of Israel. So an individual, presumably an established or rising world leader, will broker a deal with the nation of Israel that is designed to last for one "week" (i.e., seven years).[2] This peace agreement will somehow facilitate the rebuilding of the (third) Jewish temple in Jerusalem (keep in mind, there hasn't been a Jewish temple in Jerusalem since AD 70, when it was destroyed by the Roman general Titus, exactly as Jesus prophesied in Matthew 24:1-2 and Luke 19:44). However, the significance of such a peace agreement will reverberate across the world. In fact, this treaty is officially what restarts God's prophetic clock once again.

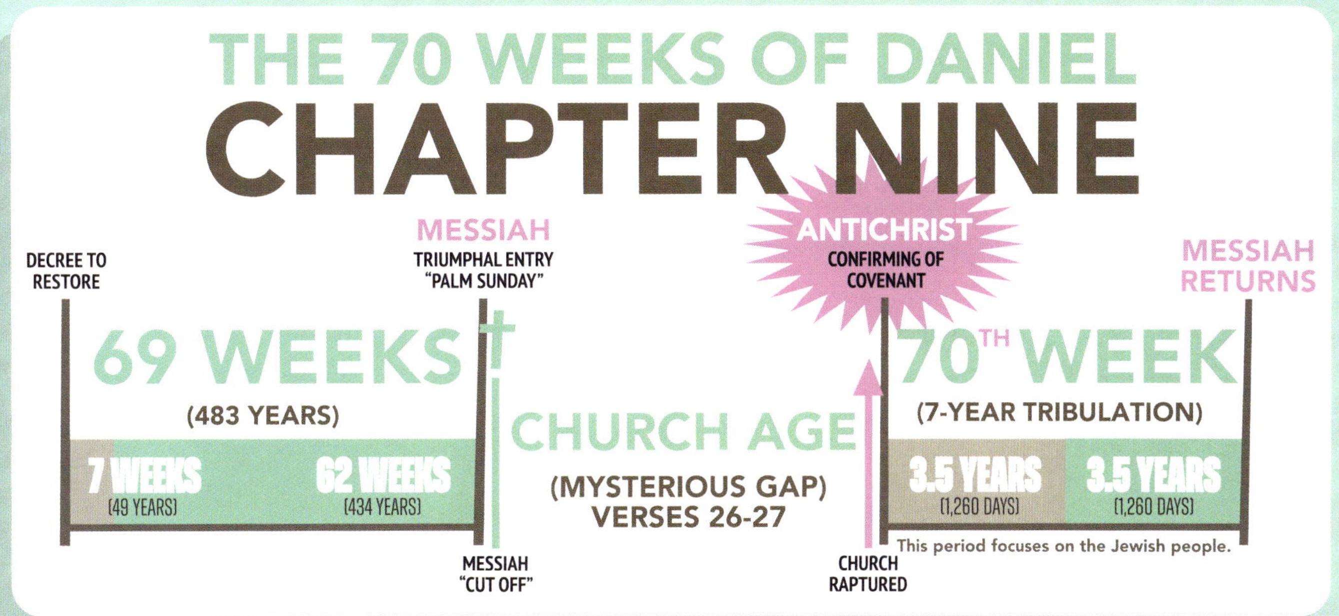

Obviously, in order for the Jews to rebuild their temple, Israel must first be a nation again and be living back in the land (Jeremiah 30:1-5; Ezekiel 34:11-24; 37; Zechariah 10:6-10). This prophecy was initially fulfilled on May 14, 1948, and is continuing in its fulfillment as Jews from around the world are returning to the ancient land of their forefathers. In fact, more Jews are living in Israel today than anywhere else in the world (6.7 million).[3]

THE BATTLE OF GOG AND MAGOG

THE PLAYERS

Bible prophecy tells us Israel will one day be invaded by a coalition of nations from every direction. It's a 2,600-year-old prophecy popularly known as the battle of Gog and Magog (Ezekiel 38–39). And the goal of these nations? To eradicate Israel. Presently, Iran and other Muslim nations surrounding Israel would love to wipe the tiny nation and its inhabitants off the world map.

The leader of the Ezekiel 38 invasion is called Gog, and refers to an individual. Gog is the name of the Russian ruler. It is a title like *czar* or *king*. Some prophecy experts also cite the possibility that Gog may be the name of a demon who is behind the Russian ruler. Gog is seen in the Ezekiel account as the main leader—perhaps protecting the other partners. His main motive will be to take plunder from Israel (most likely, gas, oil, and other natural resources) at a time of vulnerability and when Israel is living securely and at peace (38:8, 14).

However, the rest of the names in the prophecy refer to geographical locations. They include: Magog (nations from the former Soviet Union) and Rosh (the area north of the Black Sea; i.e., Russia). Ezekiel says part of this invading force will come from the "remotest parts of the north" (39:2; see also 38:6, 15). Draw a line directly north of Israel and you end up in Russia. Other nations easily correspond to modern-day Turkey, Iran, Sudan, and Libya. Essentially, the invading coalition will be Russia and its Muslim allies.

THE WAR

But how do we know this is a war that takes place in the future? Here are some reasons:

- There was never an invasion like this against Israel in the Old Testament.
- For the last 2,000 years (until 1948), there has not been a Jewish nation of Israel to invade.
- This battle chronologically occurs sometime between the *physical* rebirth of Israel as a nation (Ezekiel 37) and its *spiritual* rebirth (40–48), sometime between May 14, 1948 and Christ's second-coming return (Revelation 19).
- It takes place during the "latter years" (Ezekiel 38:8) and "last days" (verse 16) when Israel is "restored" in the land (verse 8), "at rest" (verse 11), and "living securely" (verse 14).

God will fight for Israel (verses 18-22). Gog and his armies will set out to bury Israel, but God will bury them instead. Amazingly, Ezekiel 39:9 states that after this battle, Israel will make fires with the weapons and burn them for *seven years*.

So today, Israel is in the land. The present goal that many of these prophesied nations have is to exterminate the Jewish people. Given that basically the entire Muslim world wants to erase Israel from existence, this prophecy is relevant to our time in history.

THE SEAL JUDGMENTS

REVELATION 6:1-17; 8:1-5

The seal judgments will be the first set of seven judgments (21 in total) that will occur in the future tribulation period. The first four of the seal judgments make up the well-known four horsemen of the apocalypse.

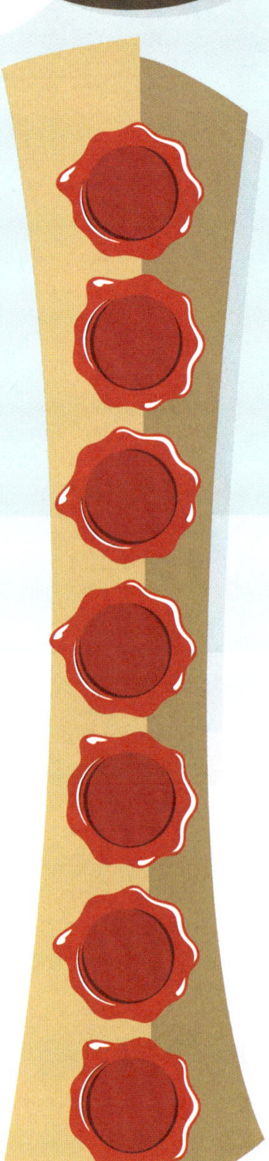

SEAL JUDGMENT 1:

The Rider on the White Horse (Revelation 6:1-2)

Sometime after the rapture, an evil end-times ruler will arise from the shadows of geopolitics. He will be a false messiah and will bring some degree of calm to a post-rapture world in chaos. He will lead the formation of a ten-nation confederacy from the region that used to be part of the ancient Roman Empire (see Revelation 13:1-2; Daniel 2:42; 7:24). This kingdom may also be composed of combined nations weakened by the disappearance of tens of millions of Christians. He will confirm a covenant with Israel to begin the tribulation period (Daniel 9:27).

SEAL JUDGMENT 2:

The Red Horse (Revelation 6:3-4)

At the breaking of the second seal, peace will be taken from the earth. This could signify various regional conflicts and threats of war that were previously simmering prior to the rapture. The Antichrist may also (in his quest for global rule) take peace from the earth as he begins to conquer the rest of the world by military force. The use of nuclear weapons is possible here.

SEAL JUDGMENT 3:

The Black Horse (Revelation 6:5-6)

The logical outcome of this world war is a massive famine. As food distribution systems break down, riots and looting dominate cities and lawlessness is unleashed. As electronic systems fail and crops and factories are destroyed by war, the worst famine the world has ever seen will lead to the death of untold millions.

SEAL JUDGMENT 4:

The Pale Horse (Revelation 6:7-8)

The fourth seal releases the pale horse of death. The conditions resulting from the first three seals leads to a catastrophic global death toll as war, famine, plague, along with "beasts of the earth" (possibly viruses, animal-borne diseases, etc.), result in one-quarter of the world's population dying. If this were to occur today, that would mean some two billion lives.

SEAL JUDGMENT 5:

Martyrdom (Revelation 6:9-11)

Concurrent with these judgments, multitudes will turn to Christ in the wake of the rapture. As people look for answers, conversions will occur because of Bibles, other resources, and the witness of 144,000 Jewish evangelists and two prophetic witnesses. However, this does not deter the globalist agenda of the Antichrist's government. Anyone found to be a believer in Christ will be severely persecuted and martyred for their faith. "Death to Christians" will be earth's new mantra.

SEAL JUDGMENT 6:

Global Mega-Quake (Revelation 6:12-17)

Earth will literally be rocked to its core. During this judgment, many of the earth's fault lines will fracture, triggering a catastrophic global earthquake. This will cause volcanoes to erupt across the globe, blackening the sky. At the same time, a devastating, massive meteor or asteroid event will occur.

SEAL JUDGMENT 7:

Prelude to the Trumpet Judgments (Revelation 8:1-5)

After the account of the sealing of the 144,000 in Revelation 7, John describes the breaking of the seventh and final seal in chapter 8. This final seal judgment will initiate a dramatic pause, preparing for the next set of global calamities—the trumpet judgments. In Revelation, the seventh judgment in each set (seals, trumpets, and bowls) unlocks the next phase of judgment and include: a proclamation (or strange silence [verse 1]), thunder and lightning blanketing the heavens, and another devastating earthquake.

THE TRUMPET JUDGMENTS

REVELATION 8:6-13; 9:1-21; 11:14-19

God's wrath continues descending on those who dwell on the earth.

TRUMPET JUDGMENT 1:

Hail, Fire, and Blood from the Sky (Revelation 8:7)

In the first trumpet judgment, the earth will be scorched by hail and fire mixed with blood. One-third of the forests and vegetation will be destroyed, and all the earth's grass will be burned.

TRUMPET JUDGMENT 2:

A Flaming "Mountain" Lands in the Ocean (Revelation 8:8-9)

Then, John depicts "a great mountain burning with fire" (verse 8) being thrown into the sea. The ensuing tsunamis and devastation will destroy one-third of sea life, along with one-third of the ships in the ocean.

TRUMPET JUDGMENT 3:

A Great Falling Star Poisons Water Sources (Revelation 8:10-11)

The third trumpet will bring another falling celestial object, this time smaller, but just as destructive. According to John, this burning torch is called Wormwood. It will poison one-third of the world's drinking supply.

TRUMPET JUDGMENT 4:

Sun, Moon, and Stars Dimmed by One-Third (Revelation 8:12-13)

The logical result of fiery meteor showers, a giant asteroid, and potential nuclear weapons striking the earth in quick succession would be a partial planetwide blackout. As smoke and destruction rise into the air, the heavenly lights created by God to guide mankind will be dimmed to a mere two-thirds of their normal brightness.

TRUMPET JUDGMENT 5 (FIRST WOE):

Falling "Star" Opens the Abyss (Revelation 9:1-12)

With the final three trumpet judgments—also called the three woes—we see a new level of paranormal involvement added to the judgments. The first 11 verses of Revelation 9 describe yet another falling star. Unlike the previous falling objects, this one is given a personality and is referred to as "he" in verse 2.

This demonic entity will be given "the key of the bottomless pit" (Revelation 9:1; see also Luke 8:30-31; 2 Peter 2:4; Jude 5-7). Whether this abyss is a physical place beneath the earth or exists in the unseen realm, the key will open its barrier, releasing thick, foul, sky-darkening smoke as a horde of demonic stinging "locusts" pour from it. They will be led by a fallen angel named Destroyer (*Abaddon* in Hebrew, or *Apollyon* in Greek). Perhaps this is Satan, or some other powerful demon. Some interpreters view these "demon locusts" as the same creatures described by Old Testament prophets, like Joel, as they describe the "day of the LORD" (Joel 2:1, 11, 31).

TRUMPET JUDGMENT 6 (SECOND WOE):

Four Killer Angels and the Demonic Army (Revelation 9:13-21)

Currently, there are fallen angels who are bound by God (Genesis 6:1-4; Jude 6; 2 Peter 2:4), reserved for a specific day and purpose. In Revelation 9, John tells us about four such angels, bound at the Euphrates River. These fallen angels will lead a horde of 200,000,000 demonic creatures (or soldiers) that kill one-third of those who are alive.

1 HAIL, FIRE, BLOOD
2 BURNING MOUNTAIN
3 STAR WORMWOOD
4 SUN DIMINISHED
5 DEMONIC LOCUSTS
6 DEMONIC HORSEMEN
7 PRELUDE

TRUMPET JUDGMENT 7 (THIRD WOE):

Ushering in the Final Set of Judgments (Revelation 11:14-19)

In Revelation 11, the seventh trumpet's main purpose will be to usher in the final phase of the tribulation period, characterized by the seven bowl judgments.

MIDTRIBULATION EVENTS

MIDFLIGHT UPDATE

Perhaps now is a good time to pause, take a breath, and contemplate what an awful time this tribulation era will be. It is a period full of God's wrath toward an unbelieving and rebellious planet. It is a time of great turbulence, catastrophe, and chaos. Keep in mind that all these judgments are literal and very real because they are recorded for us in the Bible.

We have every reason to believe they will be delivered exactly as they are described. Because of this, it ought to motivate us to warn others of God's coming judgment on this planet and on humanity. And God is not finished after the seal and trumpet judgments. There is another round of judgments that follow—perhaps even worse than the first two.

SIGN OF THE TIMES

NEWS CAN BE SEEN INSTANTLY AND GLOBALLY

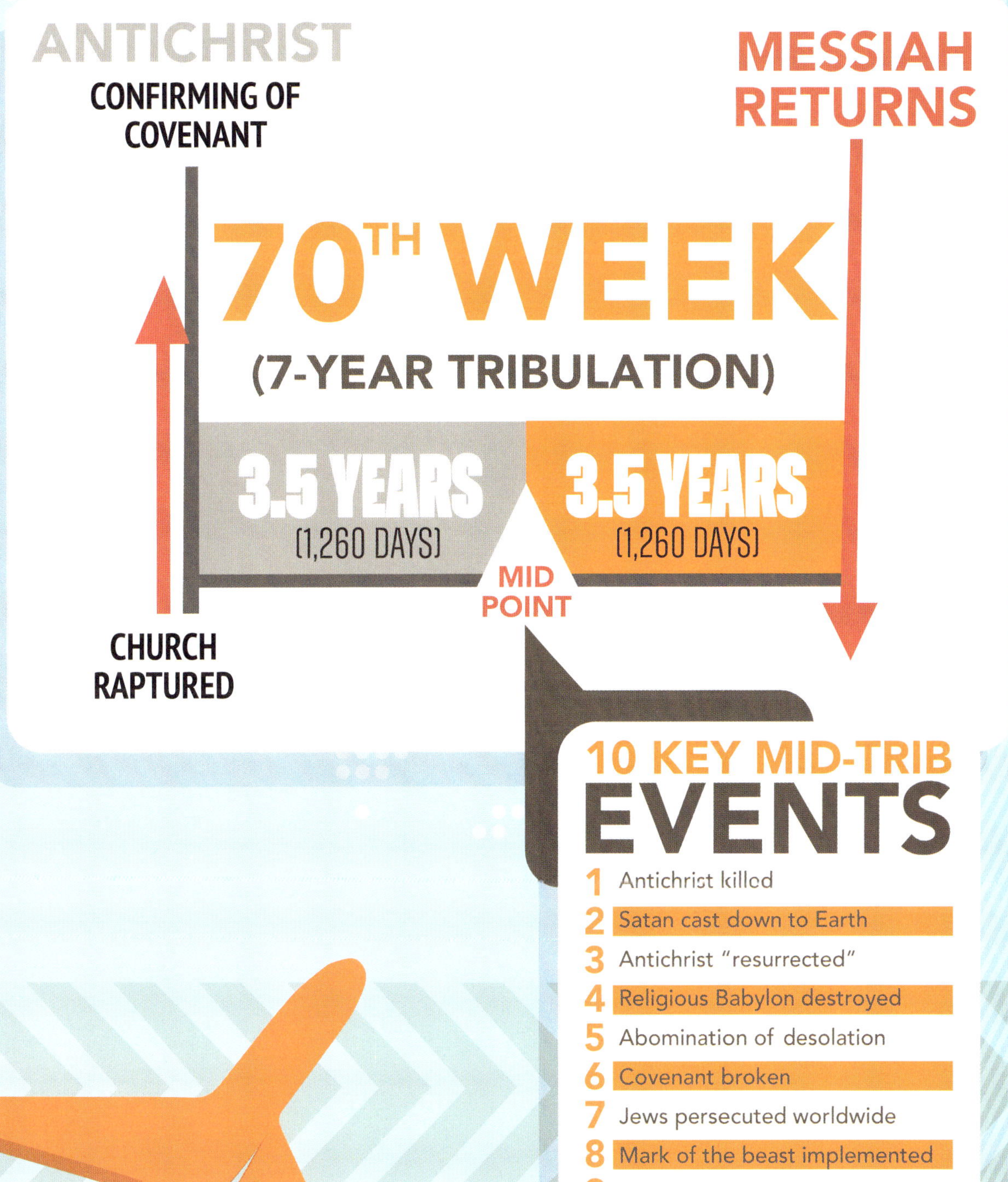

10 KEY MID-TRIB EVENTS

1. Antichrist killed
2. Satan cast down to Earth
3. Antichrist "resurrected"
4. Religious Babylon destroyed
5. Abomination of desolation
6. Covenant broken
7. Jews persecuted worldwide
8. Mark of the beast implemented
9. Worship of Antichrist
10. 2 witnesses killed

THE BOWL JUDGMENTS

REVELATION 16:1-21

BOWL JUDGMENT 1:

Festering Sores (verse 2)

The first bowl judgment results in "ugly, festering sores" (NIV) on those who will take the mark of the beast. This may have to do with DNA manipulation gone bad, some kind of malfunctioning technical poisoning, or simply a supernatural curse on their flesh. Scripture doesn't tell us the cause of the sores, but somehow it stems from the mark they will willingly receive.

BOWL JUDGMENT 2:

Ocean Turned to Blood (verse 3)

This judgment turns the entire ocean into blood, killing everything in it. Just imagine the stench! It is unknown if this will literally be blood or something akin to "red tide," when microorganisms in the water multiply rapidly, depleting it of oxygen and turning it red, resulting in a massive loss of sea life.

BOWL JUDGMENT 3:

Fresh Water Turned to Blood (verses 4-5)

The third judgment will have the same bloody effect on rivers and springs, resulting in every major water source on earth being polluted. This judgment is reminiscent of one that Moses leveled on ancient Egypt (Exodus 7:14-25).

BOWL JUDGMENT 4:

Intense Heat (verses 8-9)

This judgment seems to include a breakdown of the earth's protective atmosphere, possibly with massive solar flares or coronal mass ejections. People will be "scorched with fierce heat" from the sun; but instead of repenting, humanity blasphemes the name of God (verse 9).

We believe the first two sets of judgments will likely culminate by the midpoint of the tribulation period, leaving the bowl judgments to occur in the remaining three and a half years. The three sets of judgments described in Revelation get progressively worse. And in Revelation 16, God holds nothing back.

BOWL JUDGMENT 5:

Darkness (verses 10-11)

Again, like judgment Moses brought upon Pharaoh's kingdom (Exodus 10:21-29), the beast's kingdom will get plunged into thick darkness. And people will blaspheme God as they gnaw "their tongues because of pain" (Revelation 16:10).

BOWL JUDGMENT 6:

The Euphrates Dries Up (verse 12)

The sixth bowl judgment will dry up the Euphrates River "so that the way would be prepared for the kings from the east" (verse 12). These include immense armies from Asia, coming to join the final end-times battle of Armageddon. Next, Satan and the Antichrist will release three demon spirits "like frogs" (verse 13) that will perform supernatural signs persuading the kings of the earth to gather their armies together "for the war of the great day of God, the Almighty" (verse 14). This is in preparation for "Har-Magedon" (verse 16), or Armageddon.

BOWL JUDGMENT 7:

The Ultimate Earthquake (verses 17-21)

The final judgment includes the worst earthquake the world has ever seen. The earthquake in the first half of the tribulation moved mountains and islands from their place, possibly indicating a pole or crustal shift. But the tribulation era's final earthquake will cause entire cities to collapse. Jerusalem will split into three parts. Every island will sink and mountain crumble. And as if that wasn't bad enough, 100-pound hailstones will fall on a rebellious humanity as they continue blaspheming God.

THE FALL OF BABYLON

REVELATION 17–18

In Revelation 17, *Babylon* refers to a worldwide apostate religious system that will engulf the earth's population during the first half of the tribulation. But it's also a literal city that will be rebuilt to serve Satan's end-times strategy and be used as the Antichrist's political and economic headquarters. In fact, the word *Babylon* is used some 300 times in the Bible, and in every instance it refers to a literal city or the religious system that stems from it.

The angel with "great authority" describes political and economic Babylon as a "dwelling place of demons" (18:1-2). And another voice from heaven states, "Her sins have piled up as high as heaven" (verse 5). This could be another veiled reference to the original rebellion at the Tower of Babel. But God will pay her back "double according to her deeds" (verse 6).

This wicked city will be suddenly and catastrophically destroyed by God during the seventh bowl judgment. Though religious and commercial Babylon will indulge herself in the wine of immorality, greed, and even the blood of the saints, God always has the last word. And He will prepare a drink specially mixed for her, fermented in His full fury and wrath.

A colossal earthquake will destroy the great city in one hour (verses 10, 17, 19). The Antichrist's headquarters—Babylon—will be no more. All the chief cities of the nations will also fall at this time, as there will be an immediate global economic crash (18:9-19).

THE RETURN OF CHRIST—

Revelation 19 provides many specific details regarding Jesus' second coming. This monumental event occurs at the close of the seven-year tribulation. Many are familiar with the description of Christ showing up at the battle of Armageddon, however, may not know the actual reasons why He will return. From Scripture, we can uncover at least seven primary motivations for what will prove to be the most dramatic moment in all human history.

SEVEN REASONS FOR JESUS' RETURN

Because Jesus said He would ***(Matthew 24:29-31; 25:31).***

In other words, He's going to fulfill the promise of His word. The two angels at Jesus' ascension also prophesied that He would come back, and as it turns out, to the exact same location (Acts 1:9-11). The prophet Zechariah also predicted this (Zechariah 14:4).

To defeat God's enemies ***(Revelation 19:19-21).***

For some, it's disturbing to think about God having enemies. After all, He's supposed to love everyone, right? But Revelation makes it clear that "the kings of the earth and their armies" assemble at Armageddon "to make war against Him who sat on the horse and against His army" (Revelation 19:19). Remember, the armies of the earth will be lured by three demons for the express purpose of fighting God (16:12-14, 16). They will surround Jerusalem as well (Zechariah 12:2-4).

Unfortunately, for the millions of warriors that will assemble upon that great outstretched battlefield, it will be no contest. In fact, it will be history's bloodiest and most brutal slaughter. Presumably, not a shot will be fired. First, Jesus blinds the forces with His radiant glory (Zechariah 12:4; Matthew 24:30). Then, He simply utters a word from His mouth, slaying them all instantly (Revelation 19:15; Isaiah 11:4). According to Revelation 14:17-18, He will be accompanied by special angels and followed on white horses by all the redeemed of the ages (19:14; see also Matthew 13:39; 16:27). This is divine judgment—why it is a "terrifying thing to fall into the hands of the living God" (Hebrews 10:31).

JESUS' SECOND COMING

To regather and restore Israel ***(Isaiah 43:5-6; Jeremiah 30:10; 33:6-9; Ezekiel 36:24-38; 37:1-28; Isaiah 11:11; Romans 11:25-27).***

In Scripture, the seven-year tribulation is known as the time of Jacob's trouble (Jeremiah 30:7, 10-11). Thus, Jesus' return will represent an end to Israel's suffering and the salvation of "all Israel" (Romans 11:26).

To judge the Gentile nations ***(Matthew 25:31-46).***

Those nonmilitary unbelievers alive at the time of Jesus' coming will face a swift, individual judgment from Him. This is also sometimes referred to as the "judgment of the sheep and the goats."

To resurrect the Old Testament and tribulation saints who have been martyred ***(Revelation 20:4-6; Daniel 12:1-4).***

Before entering the millennial kingdom, believers who have died before Christ's second coming will need their spirits clothed with glorified bodies like the ones given to the church at the rapture (1 Corinthians 15:51-54). And it is at this time when the saints such as Job, Noah, Abraham, David, and John the Baptist will receive their glorified bodies (Job 19:25-27; Hosea 13:14).

To bind Satan for 1,000 years ***(Revelation 20:1-3).***

Amillennialists believe Satan is currently bound by Christ's finished work on the cross. But events of convergence and a literal interpretation of Revelation 6–19 (and of Scripture in general) tell a different story, refuting this idea.

To reign as King on the earth ***(Revelation 19:6; Isaiah 9:6-7; Daniel 2:44; Matthew 19:28; Luke 1:32-33).***

Shortly after His return, Jesus will inaugurate His 1,000-year millennial kingdom (Revelation 20:1-7).

THE RETURN OF CHRIST—

JUST LIKE THE DAYS OF NOAH AND LOT

DAYS OF NOAH

DAYS OF LOT

COMPARING THE 1ST & 2ND COMINGS

FIRST COMING	SECOND COMING
OFFERED KINGDOM	ESTABLISHES KINGDOM
REVEALED THE FATHER	REVEALS HIMSELF
DIED FOR SINNERS	PUNISHES SINNERS

TWO PURPOSES

REVELATION 19:11

1. JUDGE	2. WAGE WAR

JESUS' SECOND COMING

WHAT THAT DAY WILL LOOK LIKE

According to Scripture, Jesus' return will be literal, physical, and visible. In fact, Revelation 1:7 claims that "every eye will see him" (see also Daniel 7:13; Matthew 24:29-30; 25:31). But how can this be?

Some have imagined this event being broadcast to the whole world. Others speculate social media will simultaneously explode with live feeds of the event. However, likely it will be more *supernatural* in nature. In other words, Jesus may miraculously make Himself visible to every person, no matter where they are on the earth at that time. Perhaps in a way similar to Revelation 14:6-7, where at the midpoint of the tribulation an angel in the atmosphere preaches "with a loud voice" the "eternal gospel...to every nation and tribe and tongue and people." However it will occur, the whole world will hear Him, as people are graciously given one last chance to repent and turn to the true God. Unfortunately, when Jesus returns, the chance to repent will have passed.

Finally, the entire planet will look upon the most famous person in history, a carpenter from Galilee. Jesus of Nazareth. The Son of God. The Lamb of God. However, unlike His first coming, He will be robed in great splendor and glory. Consistent with the vision John received in Revelation 1, Jesus' eyes are a flame of fire and upon His head are many diadems (19:12). He is riding a white horse (verse 11).

Previously, we saw another rider (the Antichrist) on a white horse who "went out conquering and to conquer" (6:2). That man was a liar and an imposter. But *this* Christ is "Faithful and True" and "in righteousness He judges and wages war" (19:11). And the Antichrist will be present to witness this scene. The end of history will come by Jesus bursting through the clouds (Matthew 25:31; Revelation 19:14). Talk about a dramatic entrance! And yet, one fitting for Him who is the "KING OF KINGS, AND LORD OF LORDS" (19:16).

THE CAMPAIGN OF ARMAGEDDON

The so-called "battle of Armageddon" is, in reality, more of a campaign. In the lead-up to this final showdown, Daniel 11:40-45 describes a Middle-East military conflict that will occur toward the end of the tribulation period. After the key midtribulation events (the abomination of desolation, the mark of the beast, the gospel-preaching angels, etc.), the Antichrist will pursue the Jewish people (and likely the remaining tribulation saints) with intense fury and violence (Revelation 12:13-16; 13:7). Surprisingly, at this same time, some nations will attempt to push back against the global rulership of the Antichrist (Daniel 11:40-41).

After a successful military campaign in the Middle East, the Antichrist will enter the land of Israel. But he will hear news from the north and the east that alarms him. This *could* mean that Russia will have resupplied their military to a level where they could muster an assault (having been decimated roughly seven years prior during the Ezekiel 38 defeat). At the same time, the armies of the kings of the east (Revelation 16:12) will cross the Euphrates River, on their way to confront the Antichrist. This perfect storm of convergence will cause all these armies to gather on the most famous staging area for battle in the world—the Valley of Megiddo, better known as *Armageddon*.

However, just as earth's armies arrive in the valley, their attention will suddenly shift upward, causing them to unite against a much greater common foe—Jesus Christ. Matthew 24:30 states, "The sign of the Son of Man will appear in the sky, and then all the tribes of the earth will mourn, and they will see the Son of Man coming on the clouds of the sky with power and great glory." Perhaps tens of millions assembled there that day will witness God's heavenly shekinah glory piercing the blackness of the sky. And they will instinctively know what it means. The Lord, who has sent judgment from heaven for seven years, has arrived in person to finish them. This godless, global army led by the Antichrist will be deluded enough to believe they can actually combine forces to take on the Son of God. But Jesus will speak, and the battle will be over before it even begins.

Today, our generation is previewing the tribulation generation, as "there is no fear of God before their eyes" (Romans 3:18; see also Psalm 36:1). During the tribulation (and leading up to it), the number of hardened hearts will exponentially increase as humanity repeatedly refuses to repent, and consistently hates, curses, and blasphemes God and His Son (Romans 1:30; 2 Timothy 3:1-4; Revelation 9:20-21; 16:11, 21). Ironically, they will assemble to "make war" against Jesus Christ; but little do they realize Christ will come to make war with *them*!

ARMAGEDDON
ORDER OF EVENTS

EUPHRATES RIVER

4 ARMIES JOIN FORCES IN AN ATTEMPT TO WAR AGAINST THE RETURNING CHRIST

THE 75-DAY INTERVAL

After Jesus slays His enemies at Armageddon (Revelation 19:15), all remaining birds of the earth are invited to come feast on the freshly killed corpses (19:17-18, 21). At this time, the Antichrist and the false prophet are "seized" and thrown into the lake of fire (Revelation 19:19-20). We're not told whether Christ or an angel will lay hold of these two men. Regardless, they are not destroyed in the battle, rather, they are thrown alive into the dreaded lake of fire, becoming the first eternal residents of this awful place. There, they are "tormented day and night forever and ever" (Revelation 20:10).

What follows the second coming is a fascinating 75-day transitional period between the end of the tribulation and the inauguration of the millennial kingdom (Daniel 12:11-12).

The prophet Daniel outlines three lengths of time: 1,260 days (9:27), 1,290 days (12:11), and 1,335 days (12:12). Remember, the second half of the tribulation lasts for 1,260 days (three and a half years). And yet, Daniel writes, "Blessed are those who wait and remain until the end of the 1,335 days" (verse 12 NLT). So what is the meaning and purpose of the extra 30 and 45 days (1,335 – 1,260 = 75)? What will take place during this time?

Some have suggested this period can be compared to the gap that occurs between when a US president is elected (November) and when they are sworn into office (January). But here is what we do know: several important events will occur during this time.

Thirty days after Jesus' return, the image of the Antichrist standing in the rebuilt Jewish temple (the abomination of desolation) will be taken down and removed (Daniel 12:11). Within that 30 days, likely the temple will be demolished and rebuilt for the millennial kingdom, as the tribulation temple may be irreparably damaged due to the battles in Jerusalem, or perhaps, the impact of Jesus' "earthquake" return on the Mount of Olives (Isaiah 2:2-4; Ezekiel 40–48; Haggai 2:6-9; Zechariah 6:9-15).

Also during the 30 days, all remaining Israel will be gathered and judged by Jesus (Ezekiel 20:33-38; Matthew 24:31; 25:1-30). These Jewish believers will enter the kingdom in their earthly bodies.

Jesus judges the Gentile nations. This is known as "the sheep and the goats" judgment (Matthew 25:31-46). The judgment is believed to take place in the Kidron Valley, or what Joel calls the "valley of Jehoshaphat" (meaning "Yahweh judges"), see Joel 3:2. Jesus will judge those living Gentiles whose faith in God is evidenced by their treatment of tribulation Jews (Jesus' brothers, Matthew 25:40). Those without faith are sent to "the eternal fire" (verse 41), while those on His right "go away...into eternal life" (verse 46). These Gentile believers are not yet given glorified bodies but will enter the millennial kingdom in their mortal state, reproduce, and eventually die, whereupon they will presumably be given their new bodies (Isaiah 65:20; Revelation 20:5).

Departures

75-DAY DELAY

1. IMAGE TAKEN DOWN	30 DAYS/DANIEL 12:11
2. ISRAEL JUDGED	30 DAYS
3. GENTILES JUDGED	SHEEP AND GOATS
4. SATAN BOUND	FOR 1000 YEARS
5. RENOVATE EARTH	AND SET UP GOVT.
6. ISRAEL BORDERS	GENESIS 15:18
7. MARRIAGE SUPPER	REVELATION 19:7-9

Satan is bound and thrown into the abyss (Revelation 20:1-3).

God renovates a planet ravaged by His judgments, preparing it for suitable habitation as well as cleansing the land from the dead at Armageddon and other catastrophes. This time may also be used by Jesus to set up His government and assign kingdom responsibilities for us (Isaiah 65:17-21; Daniel 12:11-13).

The original land borders promised to Israel (from Egypt to the Euphrates) will be established (Genesis 15:18).

The celebration of the marriage supper of the Lamb will begin (Revelation 19:7-9). This will be a great party like none other!

Whatever else will happen during this time, we can be assured that it will involve great joy and celebration, as Christ has returned and is about to reign!

THE MILLENNIAL KINGDOM

After the return of Christ, there will be a 75-day interval, followed by the long-awaited millennial kingdom—which will serve as the front porch to eternity, the overture to the full production, the prelude to the grand masterpiece, the initial leg of our unending adventure, and the beginning of our eternal rest!

As opposed to the various human attempts to establish a global government—by the likes of Nimrod (Tower of Babel), modern despots such as Hitler, or the evil future figure known as the Antichrist—God will usher in the true version of a utopian kingdom. God's rule will reign. It will be truly good. It will be global. And it will be a literal government, not an allegorical reign representing the church age.

ISRAEL'S BORDERS
IN THE FUTURE MILLENNIAL KINGDOM

CURRENT BORDERS
EUPHRATES RIVER
(OR THE ANCIENT WADI OF EGYPT)
FUTURE BORDERS
NILE RIVER

Throughout Scripture we are given a great number of details about this future kingdom age. Nearly all the prophets spoke about it and David wrote about it in the Psalms. Jesus taught about it in many of His parables and overt conversations. The Epistles look forward to it. And in Revelation—the capstone of Scripture—its duration is revealed. In the first seven verses of Revelation 20, we're told six times that it will be 1,000 years.

GENESIS (ABRAHAMIC COVENANT)
2 SAMUEL & 2 CHRONICLES (DAVIDIC COVENANT)

THE CHRISTMAS-KINGDOM CONNECTION

Isaiah 9:6-7

For a child will be born to us, a son will be given to us; and the government will rest on His shoulders; and His name will be called Wonderful Counselor, Mighty God, Eternal Father, Prince of Peace.

There will be no end to the increase of His government or of peace, on the throne of David and over his kingdom, to establish it and to uphold it with justice and righteousness from then on and forevermore. The zeal of the LORD of hosts will accomplish this.

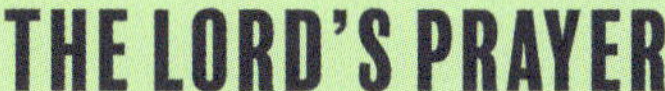

THE LORD'S PRAYER

Matthew 6:9-10 (NIV)

This, then, is how you should pray: "Our Father in heaven, hallowed be your name, your kingdom come, your will be done, on earth as it is in heaven."

KINGDOM FAST FACTS

Scripture has much to share about the conditions of the future kingdom, including details about: people (Isaiah 11:4, 9; 51:4), animals (Isaiah 11:6-9), the planet (Isaiah 2:2; Zechariah 14:8), and the government (Jeremiah 23:5; Isaiah 9:7; 33:22; Matthew 19:28; 25:31; 1 Timothy 6:15; Revelation 17:14; 20:4).

Three main purposes God has for the millennial kingdom are to fulfill prophecy, provide a period for His children to rule and reign with righteousness, and prove once and for all that sin is not a product of our environment, but of our nature.

Although it is a well-known hymn usually sung to celebrate Christmas and the birth of Christ, the famous lyrics of "Joy to the World" were written by Isaac Watts (1674–1748) to celebrate Christ's future rule in the millennial kingdom.

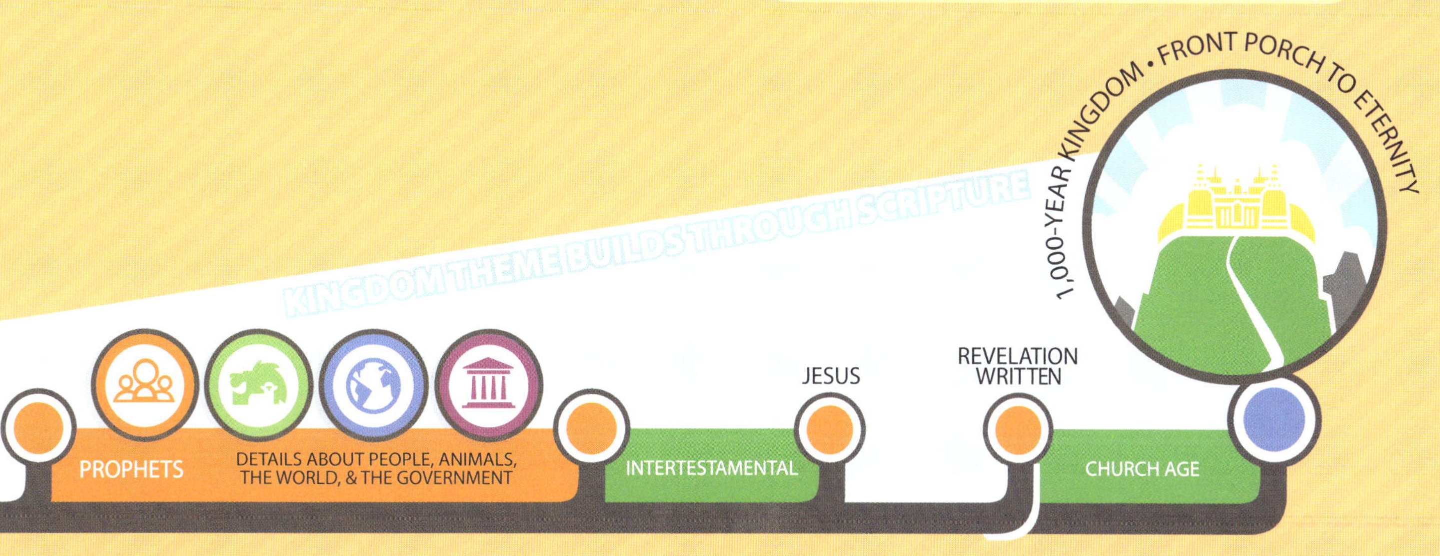

SATAN'S LAST STAND

We may wonder why Satan's reign has been allowed to linger, why his judgment has not been swift and immediate, and why he will be merely chained (instead of destroyed) after the tribulation period. But God has a purpose for everything. We see things dimly (1 Corinthians 13:12). But rest assured, Satan will get what is coming to him.

In Revelation 20:7-10, we read,

> When the thousand years are over, Satan will be released from his prison and will go out to deceive the nations in the four corners of the earth—Gog and Magog—and to gather them for battle. In number they are like the sand on the seashore. They marched across the breadth of the earth and surrounded the camp of God's people, the city he loves. But fire came down from heaven and devoured them. And the devil, who deceived them, was thrown into the lake of burning sulfur, where the beast and the false prophet had been thrown. They will be tormented day and night for ever and ever (NIV).

The great counterfeiter will mimic the return of Christ with his own second coming—another self-deceived attempt to kill the Creator. In short order upon his release, Satan will be able to deceive the nations for one final rebellion. Those who are born to the believers who survived the tribulation will still have a sin nature, and not all will accept Christ and follow His ways. By the end of the 1,000 years, there will be many unbelievers who willingly rebel against Christ when Satan is released for one last battle. This will demonstrate once and for all that mankind's sin nature is enough to cause people to rebel against God—even in a perfect utopia.

SATAN'S LAST STAND WILL BE MET WITH SWIFT, DECISIVE JUDGMENT.

The Gog and Magog description is an iconic reference to the great Ezekiel 38 war, which will have occurred more than 1,007 years prior to this event. This is similar to how people symbolically reference famous battles or wars today. For example, the famous battle of Waterloo, is used as an idiom for a tough struggle. Another example is how people use the terms *Armageddon* and *apocalypse* to mean destruction. Neither word means destruction, but the connotations are understood.

For the final time, the world's aggression will focus on Jerusalem. If these future rebels won't believe the stories of Jesus single-handedly obliterating the armies of the Antichrist, then they will learn of His matchless power firsthand. As soon as the hordes in this final rebellion finish their long trek and surround Jerusalem, fire will come down and instantly vaporize them. Finally, Satan will be punished in the lake of burning sulfur. Evil will not merely be destroyed, it will be eternally punished. The beast and the false prophet, who were thrown in 1,000 years earlier, are still seen existing in this horrible condition.

The dragon. The serpent. The devil. The accuser. The thief. The destroyer. Satan. After one last stand, finally, Lucifer will be completely and utterly punished—permanently.

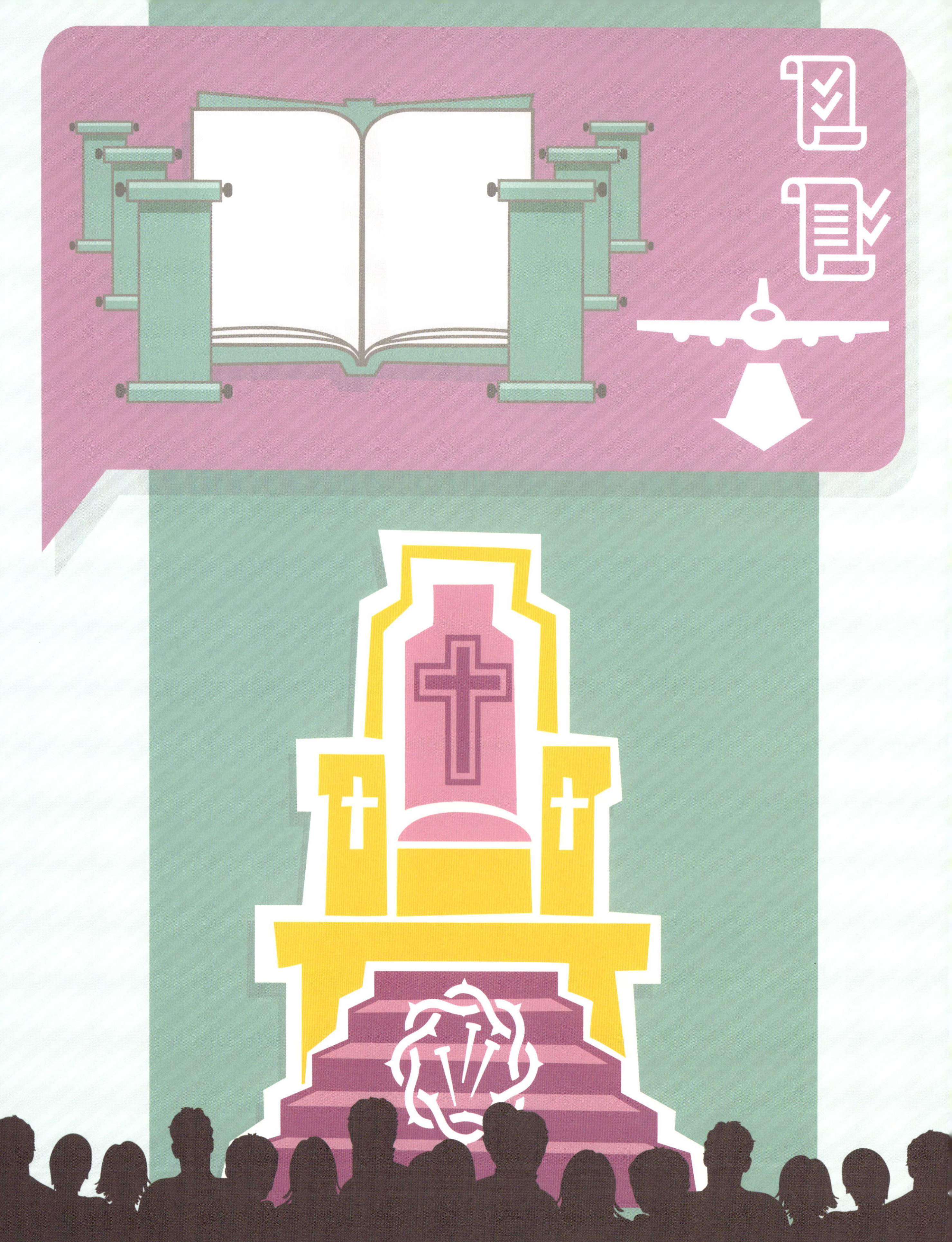

THE GREAT WHITE THRONE JUDGMENT

Following the judgment of Satan, there will be one more item of business before the official start of the eternal state—the final judgment of unbelievers. This is known as the great white throne judgment. While believers' sins were dealt with at the cross, those who do not know Christ will stand before God and give an account. We read about this event in Revelation 20:11-15, where John describes what he saw with these sobering words:

> I saw a great white throne and him who was seated on it. The earth and the heavens fled from his presence, and there was no place for them. And I saw the dead, great and small, standing before the throne, and books were opened. Another book was opened, which is the book of life. The dead were judged according to what they had done as recorded in the books. The sea gave up the dead that were in it, and death and Hades gave up the dead that were in them, and each person was judged according to what they had done. Then death and Hades were thrown into the lake of fire. The lake of fire is the second death. Anyone whose name was not found written in the book of life was thrown into the lake of fire (NIV).

In this amazing scene of the future, we see everything literally fade away except the throne and the books. Are these literal books or some kind of heavenly databank? The instances of the words *book* and *books* used in this passage come from the Greek root word *biblos* (βίβλος), and they refer to a scroll, book, or volume. The books are a divinely kept volume of data on each person who has ever lived. If you think the datacenters that governments and transnational data companies have and maintain are large, just think about the amount of data God has kept over the centuries. Every thought, action, motive, and word of every person who has ever existed or will exist is logged in God's supernatural library of "books."

Notice also that John mentions that the lake of fire is the second death. In Scripture, we learn that there are two births and two deaths. We experience a natural birth when we are physically born. And there is a second spiritual birth if we accept Christ (John 3:3-6). We have a natural death when our physical bodies die. And there is a second spiritual death that John refers to here as the lake of fire (Revelation 20:14). The implication being, if you are born twice, you only will die once; but if you are only born once, you will die twice.

God provides this future scene as a flashing neon warning sign that should drive humanity to God's grace—freely offered to all. We can stand before God covered by Christ's righteousness, or we can appear and answer for what has been recorded in the books.

NEW HEAVENS, NEW EARTH, AND NEW JERUSALEM

The final stop on our flight will be where believers will spend eternity. A new heaven and earth have been promised in both the Old and New Testaments. In 2 Peter 3:13, we read, "In keeping with his promise we are looking forward to a new heaven and a new earth, where righteousness dwells" (NIV).

God is in the business of resurrection and restoration. He will do it at the rapture, and He will do it at the end of all things. In 2 Peter 3:10, we read, "The heavens will disappear with a roar; the elements will be destroyed by fire, and the earth and everything done in it will be laid bare" (NIV). God will purge all corruption out of creation and carefully craft the new heaven and the new earth. The angels witnessed creation the first time (Job 38:4-7). We will join in their witness the second time.

The new heaven and earth will be created in absolute perfection and will last for eternity. Revelation 21–22 provides us with an amazing description of this final state. We will enjoy unending and perfect unity with Christ and experience the fullness of His blessings. This final condition in which we will live is beyond description.

Significance: Usually represents God's power, authority, and government.

Usage: Twelve or twelfth used 212 times, with the most in 1 Chronicles (26), followed by Revelation (22).

In the OT, Jacob (Israel) had 12 sons who headed the 12 tribes.

In the NT, Jesus chose 12 disciples.

In Revelation 21 and 22 we find:

- 12 "no mores"
- 12 gates made of 12 pearls (21:12, 21)
- 12 angels (21:12)
- Names of the 12 tribes of Israel (21:12)
- 12 foundations made of 12 precious stones (21:14, 19-20)
- Names of the 12 apostles (21:14)
- 12,000 stadia length of New Jerusalem (21:16)
- 12,000 stadia height of New Jerusalem (21:16)
- 12,000 stadia depth of New Jerusalem (21:16)

COMPARISON BETWEEN THE KINGDOM AND ETERNITY

MILLENNIAL KINGDOM	ETERNAL STATE
1,000 YEARS	FOREVER
TEMPLE	GOD IS OUR TEMPLE
SEA	NO MORE SEA
JERUSALEM ELEVATED	NEW JERUSALEM DESCENDS
SINFUL REBELLION	NO MORE SIN...EVER!

NEW EARTH
Revelation 21:1-8

THERE WILL BE NO MORE:

SEA • LONELINESS
TEARS • DEATH
MOURNING • CRYING
PAIN

FACTS ABOUT THE

THE TWELVE "NO MORES"

- No more sea that separates (21:1)
- No more tears (21:4)
- No more death (21:4)
- No more mourning (21:4)
- No more crying (21:4)
- No more pain (21:4)
- No more thirst (21:6)
- No more wickedness (21:8, 27)
- No more temple (21:22)
- No more night (21:23, 25)
- No more closed gates (21:25)
- No more curse (22:3)

A NEW JERUSALEM—THE ETERNAL CAPITAL CITY

The crowning feature of the new heaven and the new earth will be its capital city, the new Jerusalem (Revelation 21:9–22:5), depicted as a cube—1,400 miles in each direction—made up of beautiful translucent precious stones. In the new Jerusalem, the glory of God's presence will burst forth in unlimited radiating brilliance, reflecting throughout the jeweled heavenly city in a dazzling display of refracting color. The makeup of the city will be a constant reminder of the unity between Old and New Testament saints of every tribe, nation, tongue, and people. It will be characterized by complete harmony and perfect God-honoring community.

Many Bible teachers believe the new Jerusalem already exists and is what Jesus was referring to in John 14:2, when He said, "My Father's house has many rooms; if that were not so, would I have told you that I am going there to prepare a place for you?" (NIV).

The new Jerusalem—the capital city of eternity—will be the perpetual reminder of God's redemptive plan. The plan He perfectly carried out through the ages. And believers will call this place *home*.

- Height x Width x Depth—1,380 miles in each direction.
- Cube vs. Pyramid—Pyramids are associated with the occult and sun worship. Cubes are associated with God's presence in the temple/Holy of Holies.
- Resurrected bodies are not subject to gravity—"Streets" may include vertical passageways.
- City "blocks" may be cubes as well—The city will fit how our resurrected bodies function.
- The new Jerusalem could house 20 billion people—Even at this number, it would provide an average of 75 acres for each person and still utilize only 25 percent of the total area of the city.[4]

FULL TIMELINE OF

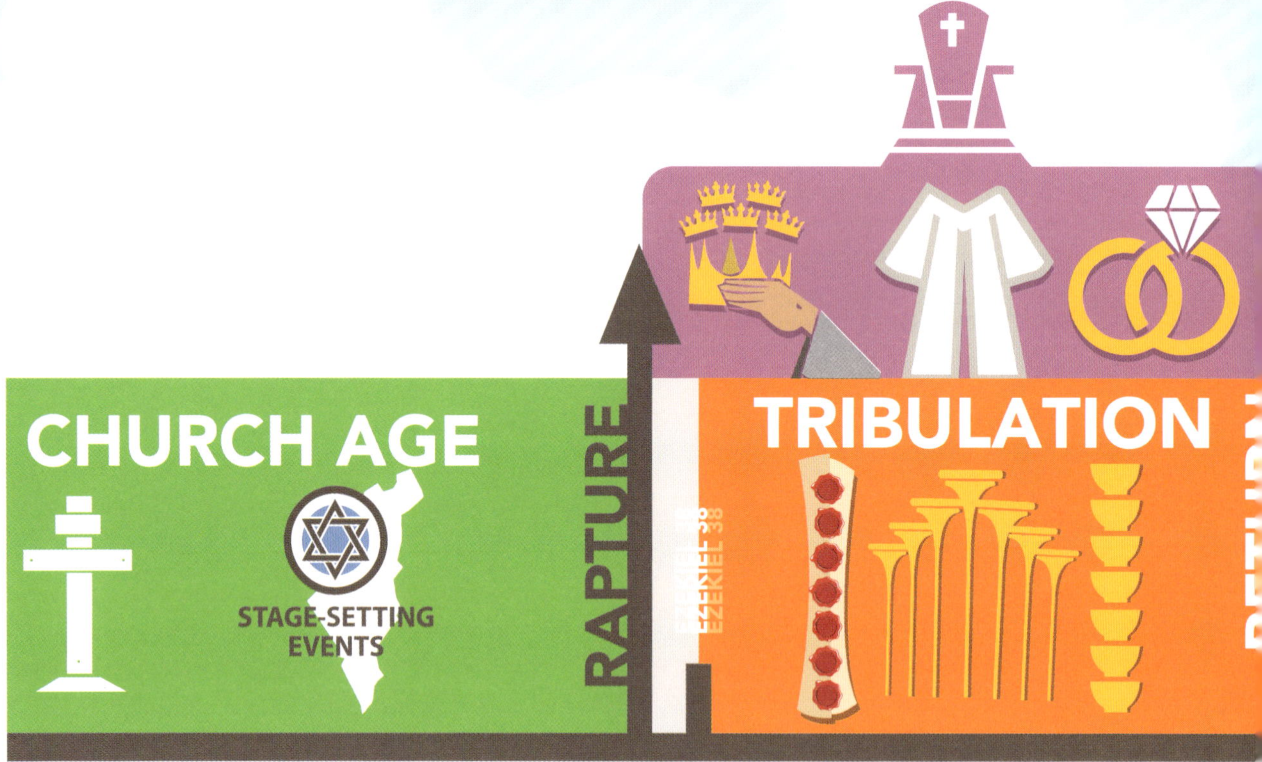

7 YEARS

THE END TIMES

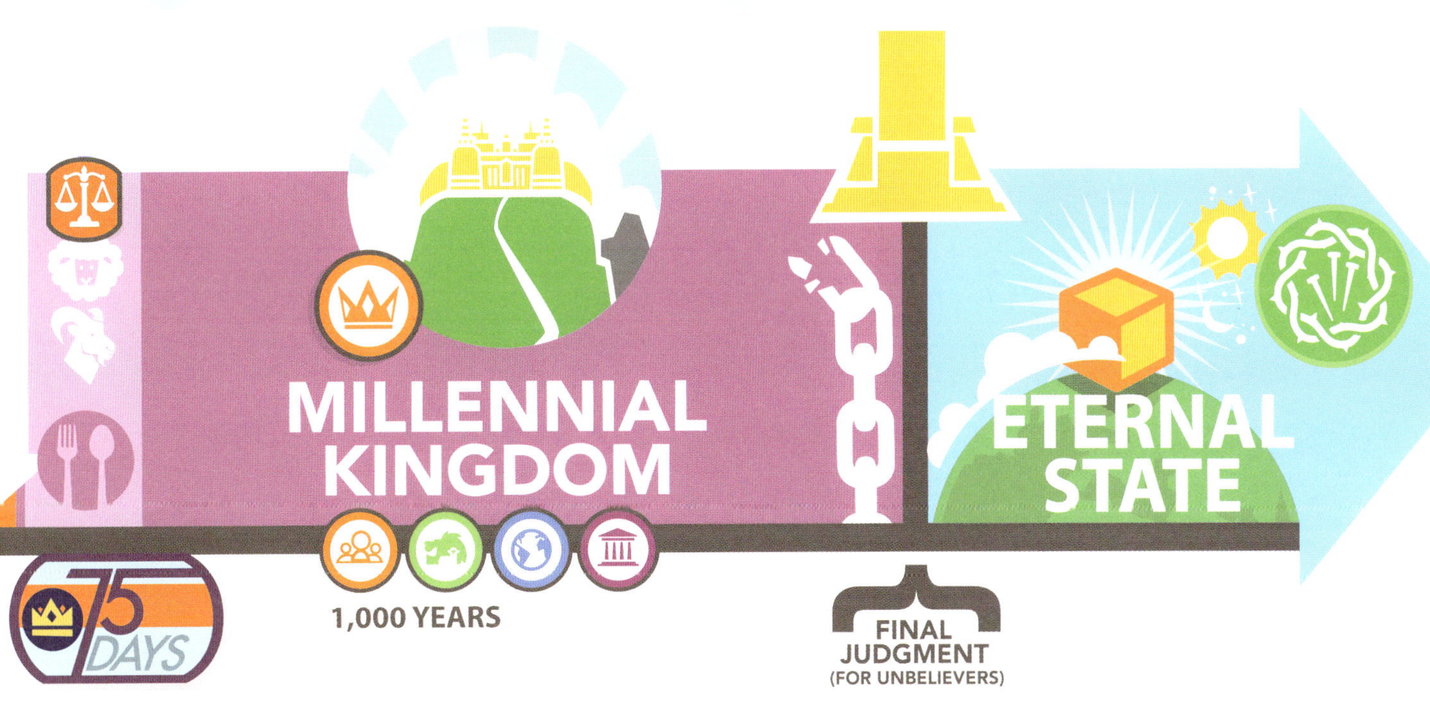

FLIGHT CREW AND PASSENGERS:

KEY FIGURES OF THE LAST DAYS

God's narrative of the last days is filled with important characters, both good and evil. It's a story contrasting good and evil, God and Satan, Christ and the Antichrist. It also involves epic battles between angels and demons (which we will see in part 4). All combined, these key players help tell the story of end-times prophecy. Let's see who is on board.

THE RESTRAINER

In 2 Thessalonians 2, Paul makes mention of a restrainer—one who is holding back the global tide of evil and instability needed in order for the future Antichrist to step onto the world scene.

Paul wrote the following in verses 6-8:

> You know what restrains him now, so that he will be revealed in his time. For the mystery of lawlessness is already at work; only He who now restrains will do so until He is removed. Then that lawless one will be revealed, whom the Lord will eliminate with the breath of His mouth and bring to an end by the appearance of His coming (NASB).

The main reason for Paul's second letter was to clear up some confusion regarding the timing of the future tribulation period—known as the day of the Lord. Due to the persecution the Thessalonian believers were facing, someone had convinced them that they had already entered the day of the Lord (verses 1-2). Paul assured them this was not the case, and said that the apostasy and the revealing of the Antichrist had to occur first (verse 3). As detailed above, Paul also assured his readers that the Antichrist could not be revealed until the restrainer was removed (verses 6-8).

QUICK FACTS:
The Thessalonian Letters

- The two letters to the Thessalonians were probably among the first letters that Paul wrote.
- They were the most eschatological of Paul's 13 letters.
- The Thessalonians learned about the rapture, the tribulation period, the Antichrist, and the return of Christ.

WHO IS THE RESTRAINER?

We believe the restrainer is the Holy Spirit-indwelled church, and that the Antichrist's rise to power will be held from occurring until after the rapture has taken place. On the flip side, God's active judgment (that is, the day of the Lord) will also be restrained until Christ takes His bride (the church—see Ephesians 5:23) out of the path of judgment (1 Thessalonians 5:9; Revelation 3:10).

Notice in 2 Thessalonians 2:6-7, the restrainer is referred to both as a "what" (verse 6) and a "He" (verse 7). The "what" is the church and the "He" is the Holy Spirit. Also notice that the Holy Spirit will not cease to be omnipresent, but His unique restraining influence through the church will be taken out of the way in order to let the end-times drama of the ages begin.

This makes complete sense considering the church age began with the arrival of the Holy Spirit on the day of Pentecost, who was sent to indwell believers (John 16:7; Romans 8:9; 1 Corinthians 6:19; 1 John 4:4). In the Old Testament this was not the case. The Spirit would come and go as the Lord willed. With the help of the Holy Spirit, each church-age believer serves as salt and light (Matthew 5:13-16), designed to hold back the decay. At the end of this age, the church (along with the indwelling Holy Spirit) will be removed. *Then*, the Antichrist can be revealed.

JESUS

If you think about it, Jesus had two parts to His first advent. We celebrate them at Christmas and Easter. Jesus' birth fulfilled prophecy, as did His ministry beginning 30 years later—culminating with His crucifixion, resurrection, and ascension.

Similarly, Jesus' second advent will have two parts. First, the Savior will step out of heaven, rapture the church, and take her to the Father's House in heaven. Then at the end of the seven-year tribulation period, He will physically return to earth on a heavenly war horse to destroy the armies of the Antichrist and touch His feet down on the Mount of Olives (Zechariah 14:4) before establishing the millennial kingdom (Zechariah 14:16).

Another parallel to note between the two advents is the unique ministry of the Holy Spirit. In the first advent, after Jesus went back to heaven, He sent the Holy Spirit to earth to officially begin the church age. With the second advent, Jesus will come from heaven to earth's atmosphere to take the Holy Spirit—along with the church—back to heaven to officially end the church age.

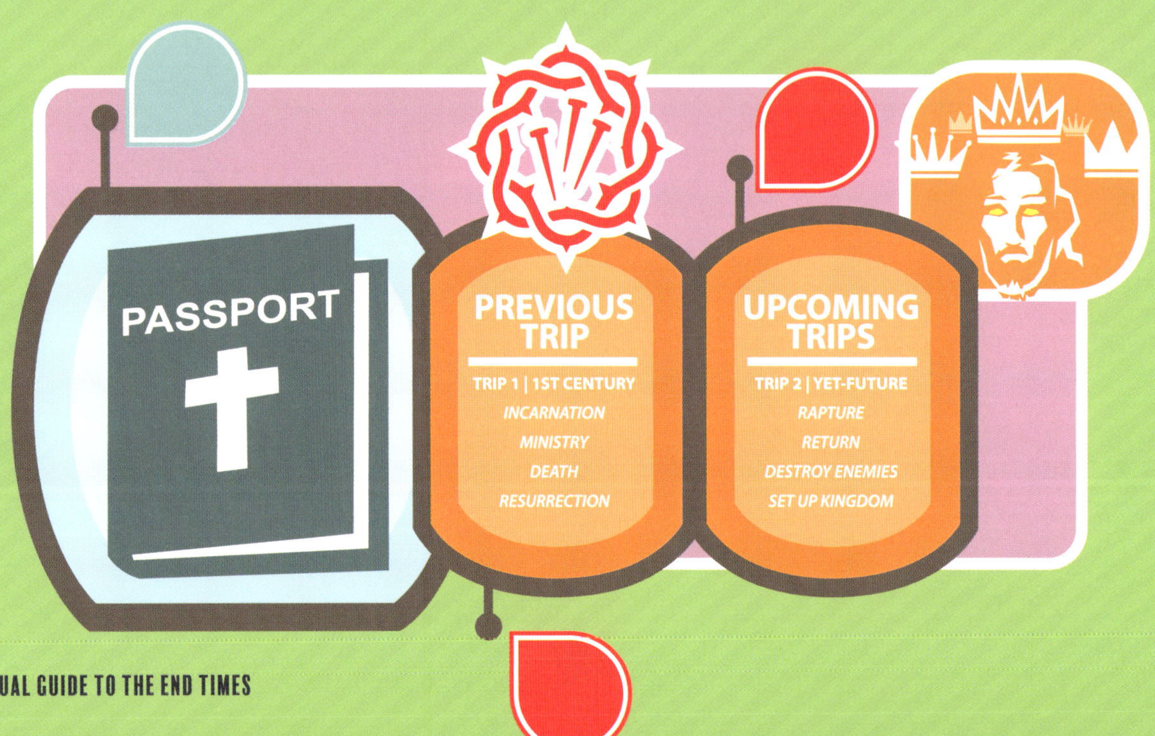

ITINERARY UPCOMING TRIPS FLIGHT 1910

Ready for takeoff!

2A: RAPTURE

2B: RETURN

THE LORD JESUS
NAME

NO MAN KNOWS
DATE

HEAVEN
DEPARTURE

CLOUDS/MT. OF OLIVES
DESTINATION

We're all familiar with the first-coming version of Jesus—the baby born in Bethlehem, the One who laid His life down for us at the cross. Revelation reminds us that these snapshots tell only part of the story. The first time, Jesus came as a suffering servant. At His return (Revelation 19), He will be seen in all of His glory—coming as a warrior-king to settle all accounts and take His rightful place as sovereign of the universe.

We see this in full, stunning view when Jesus returns at the end of the tribulation—piercing the darkness with bright glory. Coming to the world as a horse-riding warrior wearing a bloody robe and with a sword coming out of His mouth, as He leads the armies of heaven (verses 11-13).

Revelation 19:10 even states, "It is the Spirit of prophecy who bears testimony to Jesus" (NIV). In other words, the Holy Spirit, who inspired all of Scripture, put prophecy in the Bible specifically to point us to the truth about who Jesus is—in all His fullness!

Everything in Scripture is ultimately tethered to the person of Jesus Christ. The opening verse of the final book of the Bible zeroes in on this paramount fact. The capstone book of the Bible is all about the revelation—or the unveiling—of the Lord Jesus Christ in all His fullness!

In Genesis 3:15, we discover the first prophecy of the Savior. In Luke 24:27, we discover how the entire Old Testament points to Him. Finally, in Revelation, we find Jesus finishing His work and reigning as King of kings and Lord of lords. The pages between Genesis and Revelation connect all the key scriptural themes to Jesus—the anchor point of the biblical narrative.

THE 24 ELDERS

NARROWING IT DOWN

They Are Not Angels

They do not appear to be angels because:

- Angels are not referred to as elders anywhere in the Bible.
- Angels are never depicted wearing victors' crowns.
- Angels are never promised any rulership, but these 24 elders are described as sitting on thrones. The church has been promised to rule and reign with Christ (Matthew 19:28; Luke 22:30; Revelation 2:26-27; 5:10; 20:4).

Okay Then, Who Else Could They Be?

- A survey of the Old Testament shows that these 24 elders are not seen in any descriptions of heaven's throne room (Ezekiel 1; Isaiah 6).
- The elders are dressed in white, a consistent detail about those redeemed of the church age (Revelation 3:5).
- They have already been rewarded—and are wearing—victors' crowns (Greek, *stephanos*) instead of a ruler's crown (Greek, *diadema*)(Revelation 2:10; 2 Timothy 4:8; James 1:12).
- The lampstands that specifically represent the churches in Revelation 2–3 (1:20) are later found in the presence of the throne and the 24 elders (4:5).

If the sequential chronology of the rapture, followed immediately after by the judgment seat of Christ is correct (as Revelation 22:12 seems to indicate), then these would appear to be 24 church-age believers in heaven after the rapture.

Also of note is the fact that this scene takes place prior to the beginning of the tribulation period—depicted at the end of this heavenly scene when Jesus (the Lamb who was slain) begins to open the scroll (Revelation 5–6).

The identity of the 24 elders is debated. Because it is not spelled out for us in more detail, we must look to other context clues to gain insight—and we cannot be dogmatically specific. That said, the details seem to best support that the elders are 24 representatives of church-age believers.

REVELATION'S JEWISH ROOTS

But why *24* elders? Revelation is a very Jewish book. Some scholars have noted that in the 404 verses of Revelation, there are more than 800 allusions to the Old Testament. There are 144,000 Jewish witnesses (12,000 from each tribe), two Jewish witnesses, and a large number of symbols that are direct allusions to the Old Testament.

So with the Jewishness of Revelation in mind, one possibility may be that it is an allusion to the 24 orders of priests in ancient Israel (1 Chronicles 23:6; 24:7-19). The priests stood before God (in the temple) and represented all the people. If that is the reason, then these 24 elders in Revelation 4 are likely 24 representatives of the church at large. Perhaps they are actual pastors (1 Timothy 3; Titus 1). Perhaps they are giants of the faith who dared to do great things in the name of Christ—and whom we will one day get to meet and enjoy fellowship with!

THE TEN KINGS

In Daniel 2, we find a prophecy of an end-times configuration of ten toes that rule an unstable kingdom (strong and fragile). This volatile kingdom will be destroyed by God's final kingdom (2:33-35, 42-44). Then, in Daniel 7:23-24, the camera zooms in to greater detail and we are provided with more insight. There we read,

> This is what he said: "The fourth beast will be a fourth kingdom on the earth which will be different from all the other kingdoms, and will devour the whole earth and trample it down and crush it. As for the ten horns, out of this kingdom ten kings will arise; and another will arise after them, and he will be different from the previous ones and will humble three kings" (NASB).

A global government will arise from the geographical area of the ancient Roman Empire, and it will control the "whole" earth (verse 23). Ten leaders will be positioned to lead the one-world government. Bible commentators vary in opinion whether these individuals are leaders of ten nations from western Europe (the seat of the ancient Roman Empire), or of ten global regions (as has been proposed by some globalist entities, such as the Club of Rome in 1968).

After these ten kings/rulers come to power, "another" will arise (verse 24), and he will be "different." The Hebrew word used for different is *shena* and it means "alter," "change," or "violate." This sheds light on his character and his means. We saw with the first coming of Christ that the betrayer Judas was possessed by Satan (Luke 22:3; John 13:27), and it appears that the future Antichrist will be as well (2 Thessalonians 2:9; Revelation 13:5-8, 12). The final important detail we are given in Daniel 7:24 is that this ultimate evil figure will humble, subdue, or put down three of the ten kings.

REVELATION

NT

Moving to Revelation, we find a corollary passage and all the details align to shed more light on these ten kings. In Revelation 13:1, we read, "Then I saw a beast coming up out of the sea, having ten horns and seven heads, and on his horns were ten diadems, and on his heads were blasphemous names."

The key question is: When will these ten kings arise? As detailed above, it must be after a global government is formed and before the Antichrist rises to power. Remember, the church must leave via the rapture before the Antichrist is revealed. It seems to make the most sense that this evil global government, and the ten kings who rise to power, come together after the rapture, due to the current restraining influence of the church.

There will be a necessary gap period (of unknown duration) between the rapture and the beginning of the tribulation period (which will begin with the confirming of the Daniel 9:27 covenant by the Antichrist). After the rapture of the church, the resulting instability will create the perfect scenario for a global government run by a small number of elite leaders to rise from the chaos.

Gog is the title of an evil end-times ruler from modern-day Russia (the land of Magog in ancient times) who will come with a strong army and lead an alliance to attack Israel from her northern border at a time when Israel is finally living at peace and lets her guard down (Ezekiel 38–39). The country Magog (Russia) will take the lead, and protect the other forces from the rest of the nations (38:7).

Ezekiel 36–37 detail a time when the people of Israel would be scattered all over the world and as good as dead. Their land would lie desolate during their dispersion. Then, God would bring them back from the brink and lead them into their own land once again. Ezekiel 36 and 37 have clearly been fulfilled, culminating with Israel becoming a nation again in 1948—after 1,848 years of the Jews having no nation to call their own.

The next big event in the chronology of Ezekiel is a yet-future attack detailed in Ezekiel 38–39. This attack on Israel will be led by modern-day Russia, Turkey, and Iran (with some other allies in the mix, all of whom have developing relationships in our day with the three main aggressors).

This will be an end-times war, as specifically stated in the text (38:8, 14). It will take place after the land has been barren for a long time—the people gathered back into their ancient homeland, recovering from war, in a united country with one ruler, and living securely without bars or gates (37:20-22; 38:7-8, 11).

This future attack will come from the northern border (modern-day Syria, but without Syria's involvement) for the specific purpose of taking valuable goods from Israel at a time when the country's guard is down.

CHRONOLOGY OF EZEKIEL 36-48

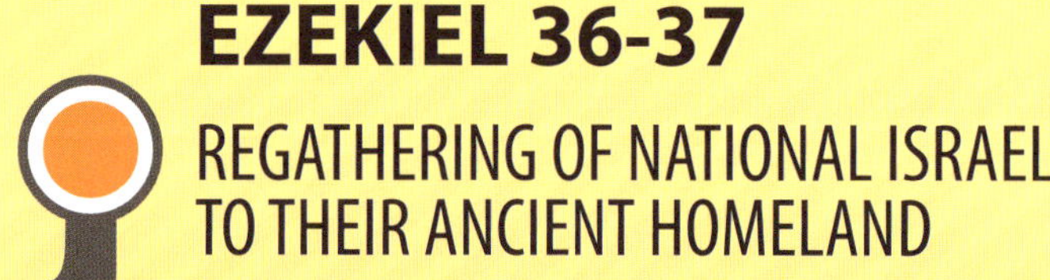

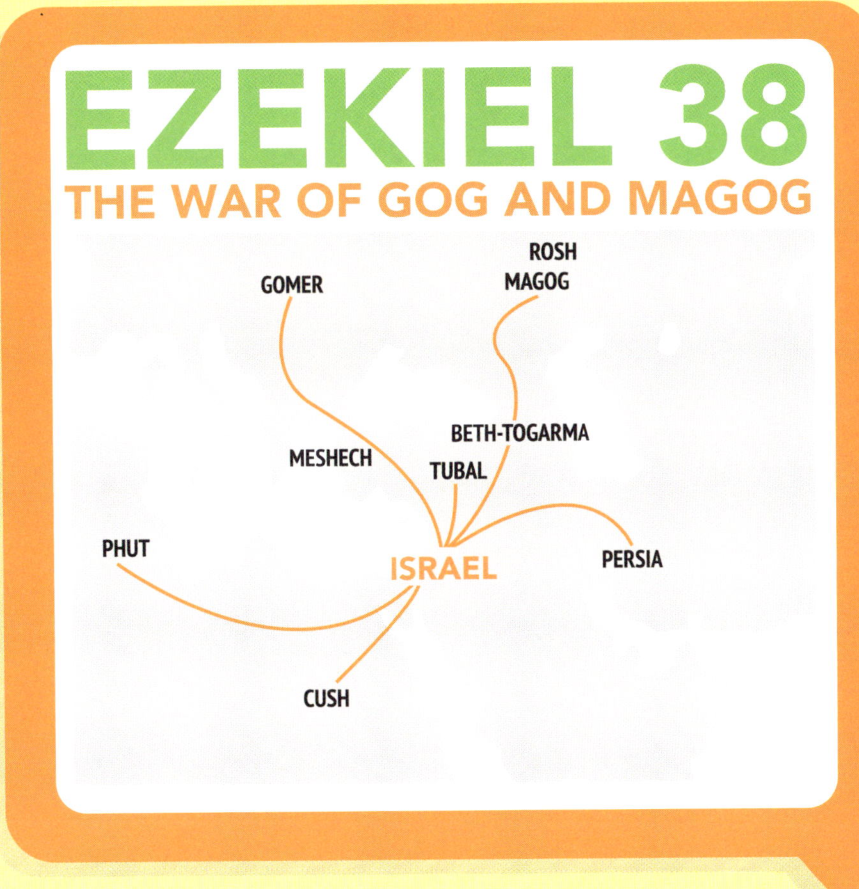

We're told that the leader of Magog will be a figure referred to as Gog (38:2-3). This mysterious end-times ruler will hail from modern-day Russia. Magog was a grandson of Noah (Genesis 10:2) and his descendants settled far north of Israel. In Ezekiel, it is referred to as the "uttermost parts of the north" (38:15 ESV). Due north of Israel, past modern-day Turkey (referred to as Gomer and Togarma in the passage) and the Black Sea, lies Russia.

The term *Gog* functions as a title, much like czar or caesar. True to the mold of ambitious and greedy dictators of the past, the end-times ruler known as Gog will attempt to use his military strength to take over a small country and its resources. But God Himself will utterly and supernaturally destroy Gog, along with his forces and allies in very short order. The plunderer will become the plundered (39:10), and Gog (along with his forces) will be buried in Israel (39:11).

EZEKIEL 38-39

END-TIMES WAR OF GOG & MAGOG

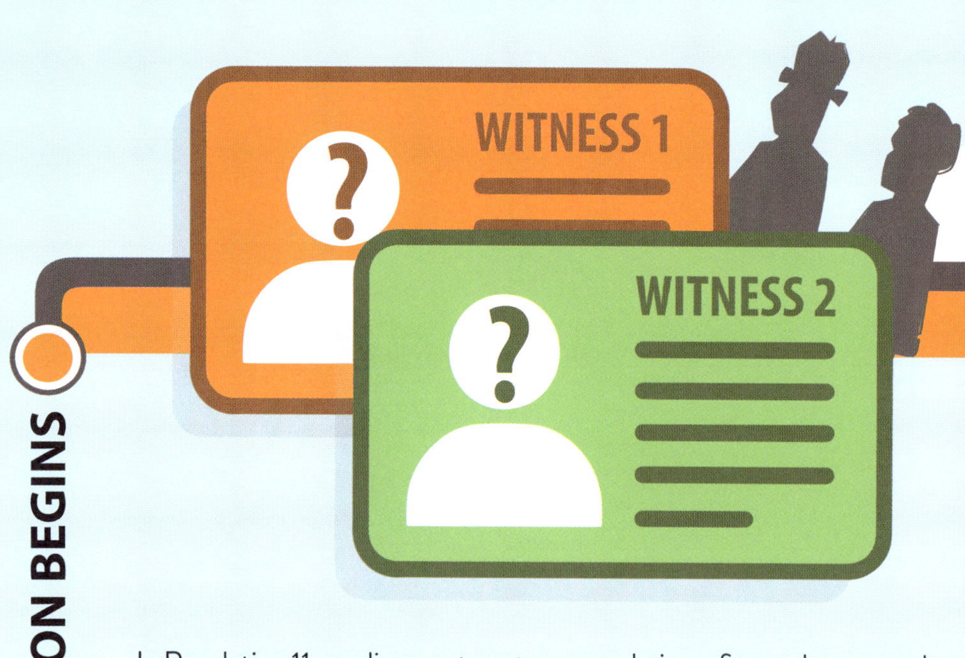

In Revelation 11, we discover two strange end-times figures known as the two witnesses. They are also called the two olive trees and the two lampstands (verse 4). We discover a foreshadow of these figures in Zechariah 4:11-14, where Zechariah didn't receive their names, but only a confirmation they were indeed two individuals (presumably, Joshua the high priest and Zerubbabel the governor of Judah during the time of Zechariah's ministry).

WHAT WILL THEY DO?

We are told that the two witnesses will prophesy for 1,260 days (Revelation 11:3)—which comes out to three and a half years (using Israel's 360-day year model). We are told that they can breathe fire and destroy people who try to harm them, turn off the rain, turn water into blood, and strike the earth "with every kind of plague as often as they want" (verses 5-6 NIV). These end-times superheroes will undoubtedly capture the attention of the world.

At the midpoint of the tribulation, the two witnesses will be killed by the Antichrist (referred to here as the beast), to everyone's surprise and delight. With the death of the two witnesses, the world will erupt into joy and initiate a new holiday tradition as they celebrate by sending gifts to one another to commemorate the Antichrist's victory over these two disruptive fire-breathing preachers. But just as the global celebrations get into full swing, God will ruin the faux-holiday by resurrecting the two witnesses and catching them away in a special rapture.

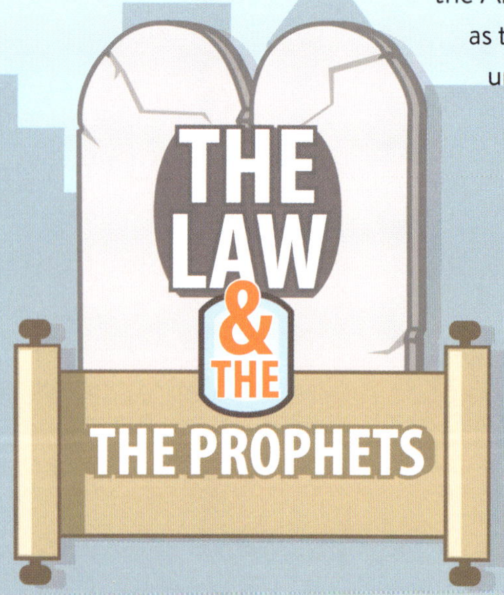

THE TWO WITNESSES

3.5 YRS

CHRIST RETURNS

WHO ARE THEY?

The text does not say specifically who these two witnesses are, so we cannot be dogmatic, but the details seem to strongly suggest they will be Moses and Elijah—the two figures who often represent the law and the prophets.

Why the Two Witnesses Could Be Moses and Elijah

- The primary focus of the tribulation period is to punish evil and fulfill God's promises to the Jewish people.
- Moses and Elijah were the two people who showed up in Matthew 17, when Jesus was momentarily changed into His glorified body in front of Peter, James, and John.
- The miraculous signs the two witnesses will be able to perform mirror those of Moses and Elijah.
- Interestingly, in the Old Testament, both men exited the scene in unique ways. Moses died and was buried by God Himself (Deuteronomy 34) under very mysterious circumstances. And at some point, Satan attempted to take the body of Moses (Jude 9). Elijah, on the other hand, was taken up to heaven without dying via a tornado-driven team of fiery horses (2 Kings 2:11-12).
- In Malachi 4:5-6, we find a prophecy that Elijah will come before the tribulation period. While at Jesus' first coming, a type of Elijah came in the person of John the Baptist (Matthew 11:14), Elijah himself will come prior to the beginning of the tribulation period—presumably after the rapture, when God shifts His focus from the church back to Israel. Jesus affirms this twofold fulfillment of Elijah's end-times ministry in Matthew 17:10-13.

In Revelation 7:1-8, we are introduced to four angels—the angels of the North, South, East, and West—and a fifth angel who will "seal" a specific group of tribulation-era believers known as the 144,000. Revelation 14:1-5 provides further details about this special group of tribulation-period believers.

WHO ARE THEY?

We are told that they will be 144,000 Jewish male virgins, consisting of 12,000 from each of the tribes of Israel. They will be sealed for use of the King—marked with His brand (so to speak) on their foreheads and supernaturally protected. They are referred to as the firstfruits (14:4), and they will (it seems) be the first group of Jewish people saved after the rapture.

12,000

Judah

12,000
Reuben

12,000

Gad

12,000

Asher

12,000

Naphtali

12,000

Manasseh

THE 144,000

WHAT WILL THEY DO?

The ministry of the 144,000 will be powerful tribulation-period evangelists that will lead the greatest revival the world will ever experience. The fruit of their testimony is seen in Revelation 7:9-17:

- A "great multitude which no one could count" (verse 9), believers who will have come out of the tribulation.
- The tough part is that they are all martyrs. Sadly, most who find salvation in the tribulation period will die for their faith.
- However, we do find that these martyred tribulation saints will have a special position serving the Lord before His throne—never to suffer again.

During the tribulation period, the world will once again see God's covenant people play a key role in global events. God's 4,000-year-old promise to Abraham—that the whole world would be blessed through him—will continue to be fulfilled in the tribulation period and beyond.

12,000

Simeon

12,000

Levi

12,000

Issachar

12,000

Zebulun

12,000

Joseph

12,000

Benjamin

THE ELITE

In every era, a select few figure out how to capitalize off calamity and funnel the wealth of the masses into their own storehouses. During great wars and natural disasters, elite opportunists callously profit greatly from crises that negatively impact most others.

This phenomenon will reach its peak in the future tribulation period. While most are suffering from war and famine during the first set of judgments, the elite will still possess their luxuries. In Revelation 6:6, we see that a full-day's work will only provide enough food for a single individual for a day, while the elite will eat to their fill with luxury items referred to in the passage as "oil and wine," which were expensive commodities in the apostle John's day.

CHARACTERISTICS OF END-TIMES ELITE LIVING

- Some of the elite will be rulers, such as the ten kings, the Antichrist, the false prophet, and those close to them
- Those who supply the rulers with luxuries are called "the merchants of the earth" (18:11)
- From these sellers, the rich will buy items such as:
  - gold and silver (v. 12)
  - precious stones and pearls (v. 12)
  - fine textiles and clothing (v. 12)
  - rare wood, ivory, and marble (v. 12)
  - spices and incense (v. 13)
  - wine and oil (v. 13)
  - flour and meat (v. 13)
  - horses and chariots (v. 13)
  - slaves (v. 13)
  - "all things...luxurious and splendid" (v. 14)
- These global trade "commodities" will include slaves of all sorts who will be trafficked at never-before-seen levels (verse 13)
- Presumably, there will also be an immense idolatry and illicit-drug industry (9:20-21)

Those who take the mark of the beast at the midpoint of the tribulation period will be allowed to buy and sell. Some in particular will prosper as they capitalize off the economic system created by the beast. Those who refuse the mark will be systematically killed and their possessions funneled to the elite. Much like the Nazis in World War II, the destruction of people groups will add great wealth to the elite.

These elite global citizens will realize fairly early (by the sixth judgment) that the tribulation judgments are not natural, but divine in nature (6:15-17). But the opportunity to turn from evil and accept Christ will pass because they will refuse to repent (9:20-21). The hardening of their hearts will continue, leading them to take the mark of the beast as an overt act of worship and alignment (13:11-18).

While this will allow them to survive and prosper for a season, the fall of this evil system will come to pass, and all their security will be gone in a moment (18:9-20). Shortly after this, the Lord Himself will return at the end of the tribulation to annihilate them (19:11-21). In hell, they will await the final judgment—when they will be thrown into the lake of fire (20:13-15). The evil elite of the end will have their moment in luxury and comfort, but they will spend an eternity suffering the wrath of God in the lake of fire.

SATAN

FIRST MEMBER OF THE COUNTERFEIT TRINITY

The Bible says that Satan was once a highly esteemed angel, but something happened that turned Lucifer into the lord of darkness. From the biblical narrative, we can surmise that at some point between creation and Genesis 3, "unrighteousness" was discovered in him.[5] This first-ever sin is spelled out in five *I-WILL* assertions made by Satan, recorded for us in Isaiah 14:13-14.

1 "*I WILL* ASCEND TO HEAVEN" *(verse 13)*

Of course, the most natural question is: *Why?* Why would an angel with such an exalted and honored position ever wish to defy God and risk losing it all? That is the question of the ages. And while much is still a mystery, God does tell us it had something to do with this angel becoming enamored with his own beauty and splendor (Ezekiel 28:17).

2 "*I WILL* RAISE MY THRONE ABOVE THE STARS [ANGELS] OF GOD" *(verse 13)*

Consumed with unholy ambition, Lucifer desired a throne and kingdom of his own. He wanted to rule over the angelic host and receive worship from them. And he nearly succeeded, as a third of the angelic host followed him in rebellion (Luke 10:18; Ephesians 2:2; Colossians 2:13-15; 2 Corinthians 4:4; Jude 6; Revelation 12:4).

3 "*I WILL* SIT ON THE MOUNT OF ASSEMBLY" *(verse 13)*

This is yet another reference to Satan's attempt to reign over heaven and its angelic population.

4 "*I WILL* ASCEND ABOVE THE HEIGHTS OF THE CLOUDS" *(verse 14)*

Satan pursues the ultimate, exalted place of universal authority. Notice the *God-ward* direction of his ambition from these verses: "ascend," "raise...above," "mount," "ascend above." He seeks to occupy the number one position in heaven, and claim its rulership for himself.

5 "*I WILL* MAKE MYSELF LIKE THE MOST HIGH" *(verse 14)*

Here is the ultimate objective of Satan's agenda. His "declaration of independence" from God. And in doing so, he makes it abundantly clear that he intends to replace God with himself. Beyond merely instigating an angelic mutiny, the devil is consumed with becoming the very essence of Deity (cf. Genesis 3:5).

We can summarize his evil intentions as follows:

- To rise above the angels.
- To rule over heaven.
- To reimagine himself as God.

And that's how sin was conceived. That's how pride and evil were born. It's how wickedness spread and ultimately filled the earth (Genesis 6:1-8). Through this act, we have insight into the core nature of sin itself. In its essence, all sin can be traced back to self-worship. Every sinful thought, attitude, and act we ever commit essentially exalts ourself above God and His authority. And like Satan's initial act, our sin is an affront to God's character and an assault on His throne. For millennia, Satan has longed to be worshipped and to rule the world. And during the second half of the tribulation, he will finally get his wish (2 Thessalonians 2:8-10; Revelation 12:3; 13:2, 4).

THE ANTICHRIST
SECOND MEMBER OF THE COUNTERFEIT TRINITY

The Bible paints a portrait of a world leader who will arise in planet Earth's last days. And we can be certain that he is no myth or folklore. On the contrary, Scripture makes it clear that he is very real, and he is coming.

The word *antichrist* is used only five times in the New Testament, and each time it refers to an *individual*, individuals, or the *spirit* of a specific individual.[6]

DESCRIPTIONS OF THE ANTICHRIST IN SCRIPTURE

- the little horn (Daniel 7:8)
- a king, who is insolent and skilled in intrigue (Daniel 8:23)
- the prince who is to come (Daniel 9:26)
- one who makes desolate (Daniel 9:27)
- the king who does as he pleases (Daniel 11:36)
- the foolish shepherd (Zechariah 11:15)
- the man of lawlessness (2 Thessalonians 2:3)
- the son of destruction (2 Thessalonians 2:3)
- the lawless one (2 Thessalonians 2:8)
- the antichrist (1 John 2:18, 22; 4:3; 2 John 1:7)
- the deceiver (2 John 1:7)
- the rider on a white horse (Revelation 6:2)
- the beast coming up out of the sea (Revelation 13:1)

The Bible also describes him as possessing characteristics typically associated with an *individual* rather than ones describing an entity, group, or a mere "principle of evil." The Antichrist is a man who *exalts himself* above every god (Daniel 11:36), *speaks* monstrous things against the God of gods (Daniel 11:36), *refuses to regard* the gods of his fathers and has *no desire* for women (Daniel 11:37). All these names, descriptions, and actions are clearly descriptive of and consistent with the person God says will appear in the last days.

KEY FIGURES WHO TALK ABOUT THE ANTICHRIST

- Daniel—Daniel 7:8, 20, 24-25; 8:23, 25; 9:27; 11:21, 24, 31, 36-37
- Zechariah—Zechariah 11:15-17
- Paul—2 Thessalonians 2:3-4, 8-9
- John—1 John 2:18-19, 22; 4:3; 2 John 1:7
- Jesus—Matthew 24:15, 24; Revelation 6:2; 11:7; 12:17; 13:1-18; 15:2; 16:13; 17:7; 19:20; 20:4, 10

BEFORE ANTICHRIST CAN BE REVEALED:

1	ISRAEL REBORN AND LIVING IN LAND	STATUS FULFILLED
2	RESTRAINER REMOVED (RAPTURE)	STATUS NOT YET FULFILLED

WHAT CAN WE KNOW ABOUT THIS NEFARIOUS INDIVIDUAL?

- An ambitious *politician* (Daniel 9:27; Revelation 17:11-12)
- A *military* demagogue (Daniel 11:28-39, 40-44; Revelation 6:2; 13:2, 4)
- A master *orator* (Daniel 7:8, 11; 11:36; Revelation 13:5)
- Charming, cunning, and deceptive (2 Thessalonians 2:4, 10-12; John 8:44)
- Arrogant, lawless, blaspheming (Daniel 11:36; 2 Thessalonians 2:7-8)
- Filled with an ancient *hatred* for the Jewish people (Genesis 3:15; Revelation 6:9; 11:7; 12:7-9, 12-17; 13:7, 15; 17:6)
- In charge of a ten-nation coalition, a "revived Roman Empire" (Daniel 2:42; 7:24; Revelation 13:1-2) with three branches—political, economic, and religious
- His pen will officially launch the seven-year tribulation (Daniel 9:27; Revelation 6:1-2)
- He will suffer a fatal head wound and miraculously return from the dead (2 Thessalonians 2:9-11; Revelation 13:3-8, 14)
- To honor him, the second beast will enact "666," leading the world to worship him (Revelation 13:16-28; 14:9-10; 16:2; 19:20; 20:4)
- He will enter the rebuilt Jewish temple, where he will proclaim himself to be God (Daniel 9:27; Matthew 24:15-22; 2 Thessalonians 2:4)
- The Antichrist's power, authority, and motivation are directly provided to him by Satan himself (2 Thessalonians 2:8-10; Revelation 12:3; 13:2, 4)

I ♥ ROME

THE FALSE PROPHET

THIRD MEMBER OF THE COUNTERFEIT TRINITY

Revelation tells us that "another beast" will accompany the Antichrist. He will also enjoy political power and popularity (Revelation 13:11-18). This man's primary role is to support and promote the Antichrist and his evil, global agenda. He is called the "false prophet" in Revelation 16:13; 19:20; 20:10, and is given the ability to perform miraculous deeds and wonders. These miracles are both powerful and persuasive (2 Thessalonians 2:8-10; Revelation 13:12, 15). He is the public relations man for the Antichrist, promoting him similarly to how the Holy Spirit promotes Jesus. His origin is a mystery, and though it is possible he *could* be Jewish, it is unlikely due to the nature of his actions against the Jews. Like the Antichrist, he too is persuasive, with an appearance like a lamb but an authoritative voice like a dragon (Revelation 13:11). He is the one who is in charge of the religious arm of the Antichrist's empire. The false prophet also draws his authority directly from Satan (Revelation 13:12).

WHAT THE FALSE PROPHET WILL DO

- Among his supernatural abilities is bringing down fire from heaven, perhaps mimicking and matching God's two witnesses in the latter half of the tribulation (Revelation 11:4-6; 13:13-14).
- He is the one who ensures that an image is created of the Antichrist and it is placed in the desecrated Jewish temple (Revelation 13:14).
- He supernaturally causes this image to breathe and speak (Revelation 13:15).
- He enforces the Antichrist's economic program by:
    - implementing the mark of the beast (666)
    - killing anyone who refuses to worship the image and the beast himself (Revelation 13:15)
- It is likely that he will spearhead the execution of believers by beheading them (Revelation 20:4).

TRIBULATION SAINTS

Revelation 6:9-11 shows that there will be a massive global revival in the early part of the tribulation. Multitudes of those left behind will repent and bow on their knees to Jesus. Apparently, these newly converted sinners are among the first saved in the tribulation. That they come to faith early on is evidenced by the fact that many of them are martyred during the very first set of tribulation judgments—the seal judgments.

Most of these converts are likely brought to Christ by the preaching of the 144,000. These men are the actual firstfruits of the tribulation, and they are sent out to proclaim what Jesus called "this gospel of the kingdom" (Matthew 24:14; see also Revelation 7:1-8; 14:4).

John declares the number of these tribulation converts to be incalculable. They are from every nation (culture), tribe (descent), people (race), and tongue (language group). It is a massive harvest of souls. A Revelation Revival! This highlights the amazing grace and great mercy of God, even while pouring out judgment.

These tribulation saints are likely a part of those mentioned in Revelation 20:4 who are beheaded for refusing to take the mark of the beast on their forehead or upon their hand.

So will people be saved during the tribulation? Yes! And mostly during the first three and a half years. But many of them will be killed (Revelation 6:9-11; 7:9, 13-14).

FROM EVERY...

AND MARTYRS *Revelation 6:9-11; 7:14-17*

THE TRIBULATION MARTYRS IN HEAVEN

- They are made righteous before God (7:9).
- They loudly and joyously worship Him upon their arrival to heaven (7:10-12).
- They are close to His throne, serving Him day and night in His temple (7:15).
- They enjoy eternal protection from further harm and all their pain and suffering are officially over (7:16-17).

NATION
TRIBE
PEOPLE
&
TONGUE

THE ANTICHRIST'S ARMY

Part of the Antichrist's rule will include a vast multinational military force. This stands to reason because his kingdom will eventually encompass the whole world (Revelation 13:3, 8; 17:11-13, 17). He will need an administration and an army to enforce his policies and maintain power over any rebellion that might threaten his rule.

ATTACK 1

Satan Persecutes Israel (Revelation 12:4, 13-14)

The Greek word for *persecuted* in this passage is a word that means "to run swiftly after, aggressively chase, or hunt down." It is the word most often translated as "persecute" in the New Testament. The Antichrist is history's ultimate "Jew-hunter." He hates Israel because through the Jews came Jesus, the Messiah. Theoretically, if he can kill all the Jews, then no one will be left to call on Messiah, and thus, Jesus won't return and Satan can rule forever on earth.

We believe the Jews' place of hiding may very well be in the area of Petra, in Bozrah (Micah 2:12). However, God—pictured in Revelation 12 as "the two wings of the great eagle" (12:14; see also Exodus 19:4)—supernaturally protects and provides for this remnant group for three and a half years.

Activities of the Unholy Trinity During the Second Half of the Tribulation

- Satan will make one last attempt to overthrow God's throne (Revelation 12:7-12).
- The Antichrist will suffer a fatal head wound and return from the dead (Revelation 13:3, 12).
- The Antichrist will desecrate the Jewish temple (Matthew 24:15; 2 Thessalonians 2:4; Daniel 9:27), after which Satan's man will launch a series of attacks on the remnant Jews hiding in the wilderness.

ATTACK 2

Satan Pours Out a River of Wrath Against Israel (Revelation 12:15-16)

During the second half of the tribulation, Satan continues his efforts to wipe the Jews from planet Earth: "The serpent poured water like a river out of his mouth after the woman, so that he might cause her to be swept away with the flood" (Revelation 12:15).

It is unclear precisely what this satanic flood will be, though John is likely using symbolic language here. It is very likely it refers to some sort of military force. See Jeremiah 46:8; 47:2; Daniel 11:26; where the same imagery is used.

However, once again, the devil is prevented from reaching the Jews by the divine delivering power of God. Revelation 12:16 tells us that the earth "opened its mouth" and helps Israel.

ATTACK 3

Satan Pursues All-Out War Against Israel (Revelation 12:17)

After Satan's first two attacks are thwarted by God, the dragon (Satan) and his false Christ (the beast) become "enraged" with Israel (verse 17). The devil's antisemitic hatred and anger knows no limits, and he becomes laser-focused on God and His people. In Revelation 12:4, he hates the Son at His birth. In verse 7, he directs his anger at the Father in heaven. In verses 10-11, he channels his rage toward tribulation-era Christians who have overcome his accusations and attacks because of "the blood of the Lamb and because of the word of their testimony." Future believers will choose a brutal death by beheading, rather than deny Jesus and take the Antichrist's mark (Revelation 13:7-10; 20:4). Finally, the Antichrist's military forces surround Jerusalem, along with the armies of the earth who have gathered at Armageddon (Zechariah 12:1-3, 8-9; 14:12; Revelation 16:16; 19:19).

THE JEWISH REMNANT

By the end of the tribulation, billions will have perished in wars and due to the terrifying seal, trumpet, and bowl judgments. But among those still standing are the Jewish remnant in protective hiding in Bozrah. All these surviving Jews will eventually call on Christ as their true Messiah and believe in Him for salvation. This is evidence that God is not finished with His chosen people.

PAUL IN ROMANS

- Romans 11:1—"God has not rejected His people, has He? May it never be!"
- Romans 11:25-26—"I do not want you, brothers and sisters, to be uninformed of this mystery—so that you will not be wise in your own estimation—that a partial hardening has happened to Israel until the fullness of the Gentiles has come in; and so all Israel will be saved" (NASB).

This "all" refers to those persecuted Jews in hiding. Every one of those remaining Jews will individually turn to the Lord for salvation. When the Jewish religious leadership rejected Jesus at His first coming, this inaugurated the period of partial hardening. But at the end of days, that hardening will be lifted and they will call upon Messiah to rescue them and be saved at that time (Zechariah 12:10; Matthew 23:39). In other words, the Jewish people (corporately) will not see Jesus until they realize He was the true Savior and cry out to Him for deliverance from Satan. We know from Bible prophecy that this will occur at the very end of the seven-year tribulation period (Daniel's 70th Week [Daniel 9:27]).

One of the purposes of the future seven-year tribulation period is for God to win His people back to Himself. Sadly, the majority of the Jewish people will reject Christ as Messiah and embrace a future false messiah (the Antichrist), possibly believing him to be their long-awaited political savior. At the midpoint of the future tribulation period, this false messiah will turn on the Jewish people and try to destroy them. He will almost succeed, leaving only a remnant of Jews who will be protected and will all corporately call upon Jesus for salvation in the end.

PART 4

FORCES OF FLIGHT:

ANGELS AND DEMONS OF THE LAST DAYS

Now we come to a fascinating place in our end-times journey—Revelation's angels and demons. The end times will see a massive uptick in the amount of "air traffic" in the spiritual world. Perhaps you've viewed a map or an app that shows you all the planes that are currently flying over the country. Sometimes, it makes you wonder how all those planes can be in the air at one time.

Similarly, in Revelation, we read about a lot of angelic activity—not only in the spiritual realm, but also materially and visually manifested in our physical world as well. Let's look at some of these spirit beings and their roles in the tribulation period. But first, we will start with a quick overview of how angels operate in Scripture.

THE ROLE OF ANGELS

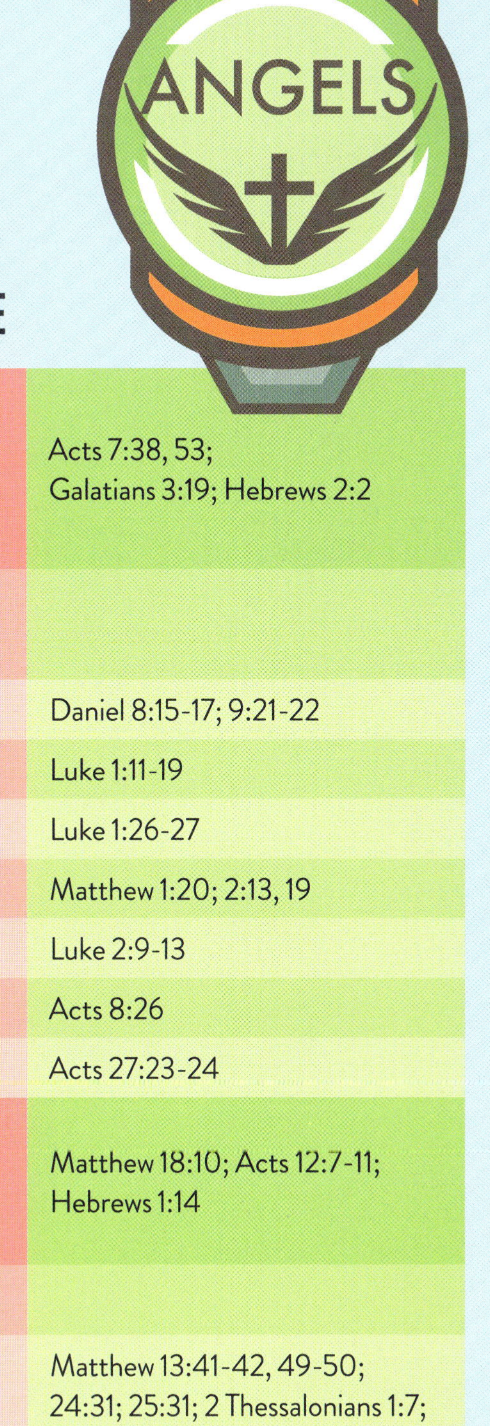

The word *angel* (Greek, *angelos*) means "messenger."

ANGELS HAVE A MULTITUDE OF ROLES IN SCRIPTURE

	Angels gave the Mosaic law	Acts 7:38, 53; Galatians 3:19; Hebrews 2:2
	Angels brought personal messages from God to people, such as:	
	Daniel	Daniel 8:15-17; 9:21-22
	Zacharias	Luke 1:11-19
	Mary	Luke 1:26-27
	Joseph	Matthew 1:20; 2:13, 19
	shepherds	Luke 2:9-13
	Philip	Acts 8:26
	Paul	Acts 27:23-24
	**Good angels care for, and minister to, believers**	Matthew 18:10; Acts 12:7-11; Hebrews 1:14
	**Angels play major roles in:**	
	end-times events	Matthew 13:41-42, 49-50; 24:31; 25:31; 2 Thessalonians 1:7; Revelation 19:14
	assisting in pouring out God's wrath during the tribulation. But also note, there is plenty of demonic activity during this time, as we see in the trumpet judgments.	Revelation 8:6; 11:15; 16:1

THE RAPTURE ARCHANGEL

In 1 Thessalonians 4, we read a play-by-play, slow-motion account of what will happen at the moment of the rapture (covered in detail earlier in this book). In verse 16, one of the details is that after the Lord shouts, we will hear "the voice of the archangel."

Archangels or "chief angels" are leaders to other lower-rank angels, and they serve God by carrying out His decrees and purposes. Archangels seem to be lower in rank than Cherubim and Seraphim (based on Ezekiel 28:14 and Jude 9), but higher in rank than the rest of the angelic beings.

The term *archangel* is only used twice in Scripture—1 Thessalonians 4:16 and Jude 9. Daniel 10:13 informs us that Michael the archangel is "one of the chief princes." Michael seems to be the military commander of the Lord's armies (Revelation 12:7) and the protector of the Jewish people (Daniel 12:1).

Could Michael the archangel also protect the church, or does the church have its own archangel? One day we will know for sure. In the meantime, we eagerly await a shout from the Lord, the voice of an archangel, and a heavenly trumpet blast.

THE THRONE GUARDIANS

Cherubim and Seraphim are depicted as very high-ranking throne guardians—perhaps the highest ranking among the heavenly beings. Ezekiel 28:14 informs us that Satan was a cherub, describing him as "the anointed cherub who covers."

Cherubim and Seraphim are strange multifaceted hybrid creatures (see Ezekiel 1:5-14), usually described in the context of guarding God's throne and holiness. Seraphim have six wings (Isaiah 6:2) and cherubim have four wings. Seraphim are also referred to in Revelation as "the four living creatures" (Revelation 4). In Ezekiel, Cherubim are also seen described as God's mobile throne drivers (Ezekiel 10). These creatures are like God's top-tier secret service agents—stationed around the holy throne of God.

In John's throne room vision found in Revelation 4, we discover that these throne guardians praise God unceasingly as they say, "Holy, holy, holy is the Lord God, the Almighty, who was and who is and who is to come."

But at a point in the future, when Jesus is found worthy to open the scroll and begin the judgments of the tribulation period, they (along with the 24 elders) will sing a new song with these lyrics:

> Worthy are You to take the scroll and to break its seals; for You were slaughtered, and You purchased people for God with Your blood from every tribe, language, people, and nation. You have made them into a kingdom and priests to our God, and they will reign upon the earth.

What an amazing moment that will be to witness as believers!

THE SEVEN TRUMPET ANGELS

In Revelation 8:6–9:19 and 11:15-19, we are provided details about the seven trumpet judgments of the tribulation period. We're given another back-and-forth view of what will happen in heaven and how it will affect events on the earth during the second set of judgments.

The seventh seal judgment will introduce the trumpet judgments (8:1), where John indicates there will be seven angels who stand before God and are given seven trumpets (8:2). This heavenly brass band prepares to play their end-times tune (8:6), which will be played one trumpet blast at a time in sequential order by the seven throne room angels.

TRUMPET ANGEL 1

Horn Blast: Hail, fire, and blood burns one-third of the earth, one-third of the trees, and all of the earth's grass

TRUMPET ANGEL 2

Horn Blast: Large flaming object crashes into the sea, one-third of which turns to blood killing one-third of sea life and destroying one-third of all ships

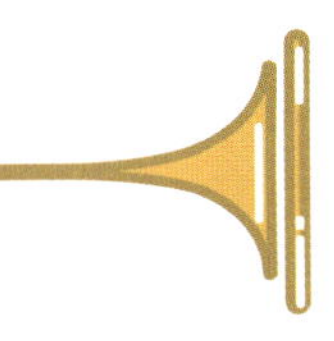

TRUMPET ANGEL 3

Horn Blast: A shooting star strikes earth, poisoning one-third of the earth's river-and-spring water supply—killing many

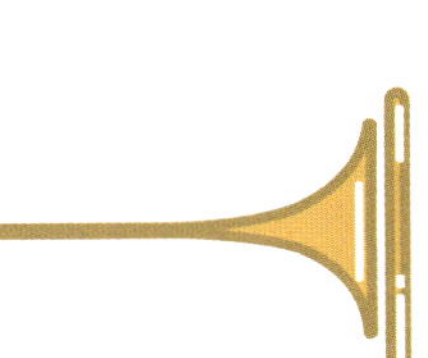

TRUMPET ANGEL 4

Horn Blast: Sun, moon, and stars dimmed by one-third (presumably from the atmospheric conditions from the first through third trumpet judgments)

TRUMPET ANGEL 5—FIRST WOE

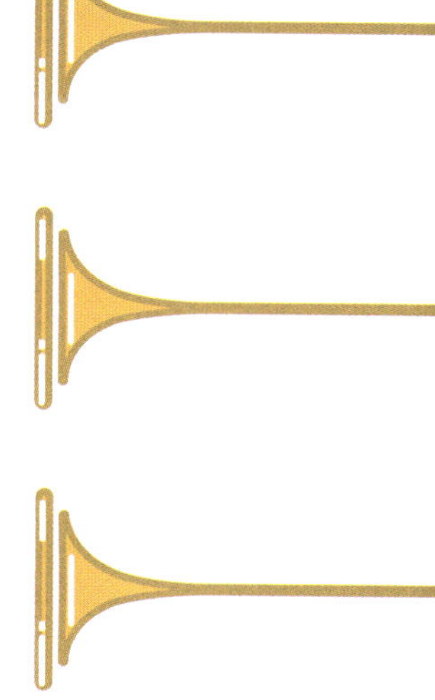

Horn Blast: Fallen angel opens the abyss, releasing demonic locusts who sting for five months

TRUMPET ANGEL 6—SECOND WOE

Horn Blast: Four "angels" released to kill one-third of mankind with a 200,000,000-strong demonic cavalry

TRUMPET ANGEL 7—THIRD WOE

Horn Blast: Loud heavenly declaration, worship from the 24 elders, followed by lightning, thunder, an earthquake, and a severe hailstorm on earth

THE DESTROYER

The first 11 verses of Revelation 9 describe a falling star. Unlike the previous falling objects in Revelation, this one is given personality. In verse 2, it is referred to as "he." This "fallen star" will be given the key to open the abyss. Angels are occasionally referred to as stars in Scripture (Job 38:4-7). This fallen angel could be Satan himself (Isaiah 14:12; Ezekiel 28:15; Luke 10:18), or perhaps another high-ranking fallen angel—an underling of Satan. Commentaries vary on this issue.

Whoever it is, this "angel of the abyss" is referred to by John in both Hebrew and Greek. In Hebrew as *Abaddon* ("destruction") and in Greek as *Apollyon* ("one who destroys"). He is the king of the demonic locusts.

A BRIEF COMPARISON OF JOEL 2 AND REVELATION 9

- Joel 2:1-11 and Revelation 9:1-11 are the key texts to compare.
- Joel indicates a shift to a future tribulation-period event (2:1-11).
- Joel mentions this is a once-in-history event (2:2).
- Joel mentions clouds of blackness (2:2) and Revelation mentions smoke (9:2-3).
- Both Joel and Revelation mention the creatures appear as horses (Joel 2:4; Revelation 9:7).
- Both Joel and Revelation mention the locusts are prepared for battle (Joel 2:7-11; Revelation 9:7).
- Joel provides limited information, but Revelation gives many more details.

DEMONIC LOCUSTS OF THE ABYSS

The king of the demonic locusts will be "given the key to the shaft of the abyss." The term *abyss* used in this passage is understood to be a temporary prison where some fallen, evil entities are held (see Luke 8:30-31; 2 Peter 2:4; Jude 5-7). It is where Satan will be bound during the future millennial kingdom (Revelation 20:1-3). Whether this abyss is a physical place beneath the earth's crust or exists in the unseen realm, the "key" will crack open the barrier, releasing a thick, foul, sky-darkening smoke as a horde of demonic "locusts" pour through.

These locusts from the abyss will be given the power to hurt people with a terrible and lasting scorpion-like sting for a period of five months. Joel 2 also describes these terrible creatures that will invade earth during the tribulation period.

THE FOUR ANGELS OF THE EUPHRATES

REVELATION 9:13-15

John hears a voice coming from the altar before God that commands the sixth angel to release the "four angels" who've been bound at the Euphrates River. This is the geographical area where the origin of sin, murder, the Tower of Babel, and a one-world government was first attempted—globalism. These are actually demons, as righteous angels are never "bound."[7] These four may be the demons who once empowered the kingdoms of Babylon, Medo-Persia, Greece, and Rome (see Daniel 10:13—the "Prince of Persia"). These angels were "prepared" ahead of time, much as the great fish was "appointed" to swallow Jonah (Jonah 1:17). This tells us that God is sovereign over both demons and nature, even able to use evil to fulfill His righteous purposes.

These particular demons have been held captive specifically for this very day, and they are released upon the earth (Revelation 9:15). Their mission is to kill another one-third of mankind. At this point in the tribulation, a little more than half of the earth's population has been destroyed![8]

Not since the days of Noah has God poured out such wrath on humanity.

THE DEMONIC CAVALRY

The four demonic generals of the Euphrates will lead an army incomprehensibly numbered at *200,000,000*. John reaffirms this truth by stating that he actually "heard" the number with his own ears (Revelation 9:16).

Some scholars have interpreted this army as referring to China because, for decades, China has boasted of fielding a military force this size. However, because of John's regular use of plain, literal language in Revelation, it is more likely they are not ordinary men and horses, as they're associated with demons. This mounted cavalry wear supernatural armor characterized by fire, sulfur, and brimstone.[9] These fire-breathing demon horses have tails like serpents, designed to harm mankind with supernatural snake bites (verses 18-19).

Those who happen to survive this horrific attack do not repent of their sins, but instead stubbornly refuse to repent (9:20-21). Even though half the world has been destroyed, they are still not convinced of their need for a Savior. Instead, they choose to harden their hearts and "worship demons," along with idols made of gold, silver, brass, stone, and wood.

IDOL WORSHIP

Idols are often associated with demonic worship in Scripture.[10] This is why the first of God's Ten Commandments was, "You shall have no other gods before Me," which is immediately followed by "You shall not make for yourself an idol...You shall not worship them or serve them" (Exodus 20:3-5).

Keep in mind, the restrainer will be absent, having been removed at the rapture. As such, demons will have a field day. Their influence and ability to oppress humans will exponentially increase. It's ironic that unbelievers will likely worship the very demons who bring some of their pain and suffering. But this is the deceptive nature of sin, Satan, and the human heart (Jeremiah 17:9).

The Cavalry's Deadly Plagues

1. ***Fire***—burned to death
2. ***Smoke***—asphyxiation
3. ***Brimstone***—sulfurous, burning rock (see also Genesis 19:24; Luke 17:29)

OF 200,000,000 REVELATION 9:15-21

HUMANITY'S UNREPENTANCE

1. ***Murder***—The murder rate will soar as chaos and hate envelops the planet (Matthew 24:12).
2. ***Sorceries***—The Greek word used here is *pharmakon*, and can signify anything from poisons, amulets, charms, drugs, magic spells, witchcraft, or any enchanting objects.[11] Drugs were used heavily in first-century sorcery, inducing a psychological state conducive to trances for contacting departed or demonic spirits. This type of drug use will likely become a global epidemic in the last days.[12]
3. ***Immorality***—Unrestrained sexual deviance will mark the tribulation generation, just as it did in Noah's day and in Sodom and Gomorrah.[13] Decency and Judeo-Christian morality will be all but gone. In their place will be a host of depraved sexual sins, soaking the earth in further defilement.
4. ***Theft***—Crime waves will reach historic levels. Lawlessness will run rampant in the streets.

The Plagues of Revelation

- 11:6
- 15:1, 6, 8
- 16:9, 21
- 19:18, 20
- 18:4, 8
- 21:9
- 22:18

WHAT CAN WE LEARN FROM ALL THIS?

- Humanity isn't getting better, but will only become more sinful and depraved following the rapture (Jeremiah 17:9; 2 Thessalonians 2:10-12; Revelation 16:10-11).
- People's sin in the tribulation era will foster a global violent spirit of hatred toward God (Revelation 16:10-11).
- God's judgments in Revelation become increasingly more acute and severe.
- In His sovereignty, God even uses demons to accomplish His purposes.

200,000,000

You can think of chapters 10–14 of Revelation as a sort of pause or parenthesis. These chapters don't advance the narrative chronologically. They serve as a prelude to the final set of judgments. In Revelation 10, God's sovereignty over earthly affairs in the last days is reinforced. The angel here is described as "another angel," meaning he is like the other angels yet has a special responsibility.

MIGHTY ANGEL'S CHARACTERISTICS

- He is clothed with a "cloud," likely referring to his angelic majesty and glory.
- There is a rainbow around his head and his face is "like the sun," reflecting the glory of God.
- His feet are like pillars of fire, speaking of the judgment he represents.
- His right foot is on sea and his left foot is on land. This points to the great authority this giant angel is given.
- His voice is loud like a lion's roar, one that commands authority.
- In his (left) hand he holds a little scroll that is open.

The angel's description is followed by seven separate peals of thunder that contain seven messages. John apparently understands these messages and is about to write them down when he is told not to do so. For some reason, those messages are for John's ears only. This highlights the fact that God has secrets concerning the tribulation—and that's okay (Deuteronomy 29:29; Daniel 8:26; 12:9; 2 Corinthians 12:4).

Then the angel swears by God, who is eternal (Revelation 1:17-18; 4:9-10; 15:7) and Creator (4:11; 14:6-7). He announces that "there will be no more delay" (10:6 NIV). In other words, nothing can prevent the rapid succession of remaining judgments. This officially signals the final outpouring of God's wrath on earth and its inhabitants. It also signifies that the "mystery of God is finished" (verse 7).

What could this mystery refer to?

THE MIGHTY LAND, SEA, AND AIR ANGEL

REVELATION 10:1-11

MAIN TOPICS OF REVELATION'S "PARENTHETICAL" CHAPTERS

- Chapter 10 – The angel with a scroll
- Chapter 11 – The two witnesses
- Chapter 12 – Satan is cast down and Jews are persecuted
- Chapter 13 – The Antichrist and false prophet take control
- Chapter 14 – The 144,000 and a preview to Armageddon

MYSTERIES IN SCRIPTURE

In Scripture, a mystery is not an unsolvable riddle, but rather, something that simply has not yet been revealed. Among the mysteries mentioned in the Bible are:

- The mystery of the kingdom (Matthew 13:11)
- The mystery of Israel's blindness (Romans 11:25)
- The mystery of the rapture (1 Corinthians 15:51)
- The mystery of lawlessness (2 Thessalonians 2:7)
- The mystery of His will (Ephesians 1:9-10)
- The mystery of the church (Ephesians 3:8-9; Romans 16:25-26)
- The mystery of Christ in you (Colossians 1:25-27)
- The mystery of Christ and the church/marriage (Ephesians 5:32)

In Revelation 10, likely the mystery is that evil is destroyed, and/or that God's kingdom has finally come and that He will rule forever (cf 11:15). This mystery was preached to His servants the prophets—the kingdom of God on earth. In this coming kingdom, every Jew will know the Lord (Jeremiah 31:33-34). It's the same kingdom Jesus told His disciples to pray for in the Lord's Prayer (Matthew 6:10).

John is told to take the scroll (book) from the angel and to eat it. The angel says it will be sweet in his mouth because of God's promises, sovereignty, kingdom, comfort, and grace (Psalm 19:9-10; Jeremiah 15:16-18). But then, it will become bitter in his stomach, referencing the judgments that are coming.

By eating it, John accepts all the Word of God as we do, the bitter with the sweet. The scroll is God's Word, and it is both delightful and disturbing, comforting and corrective (Hebrews 4:12; 2 Timothy 3:16-17; Psalms 19:9-10; 119:103). Following this, John must "prophesy again concerning many peoples and nations and tongues and kings" (Revelation 10:11).

THE MICHAEL ARCHANGEL

REVELATION 12:1-12

Revelation 12 has been called the most symbolic chapter in the entire book of Revelation. In it we see a woman, the sun, the moon, a crown, stars, and a child (verses 1-2). There is a dragon with seven heads and ten horns, along with more stars (verses 3-4).

The dragon (Satan) attempted to devour the child (Jesus), who is prophesied to one day rule the nations (verse 5). But Christ was victorious and was eventually raptured (*harpazo*) up to heaven and His throne (see 1 Thessalonians 4:17). Meanwhile, on earth during the tribulation, Satan once again attempts a coup on heaven and God's throne. That is when Michael the archangel is called in.

Michael and Satan have known each other from the beginning. This strong angel is the protector of Israel (Daniel 12:1). And in Jude 9, we learn that he and the devil argued over the body of Moses (see also Deuteronomy 34:5-6).

The only other reference to an archangel is in 1 Thessalonians 4:16. This may or may not be Michael, as he is called "*one* of the chief princes" (Daniel 10:13). Could there also be a protective archangel who watches over the church as well?

In Revelation 12:9, Michael successfully casts Satan out of heaven and down to the earth. The devil's fallen demons join him. And as we've seen, he unleashes his greatest wrath upon the Jewish people during the second half of the tribulation (verses 12-17). This is his final assault, "knowing that he has only a short time" (i.e., three and a half years, or 42 months [verse 12]).

SATAN VS. DEVIL

Revelation 12:9

- The name devil is from the Greek word *diabolos*. It means "slanderer" or "accuser."
- The name Satan is from the Greek word *satanas*. It means "adversary."
- See also 1 John 5:19; 2 Corinthians 4:4; 11:1-3.

THE GOSPEL ANGEL

REVELATION 14:6-7

At the midpoint of the tribulation, Satan—through the Antichrist and the false prophet—enacts and enforces the "mark of the beast" or "666" (Revelation 13:15-18). It is also at this time when God offers salvation one last time to the nations. And He does it through a special "gospel" angel.

This angel flies in midheaven—in the atmosphere directly above the earth (8:13; 19:17). And he is visible to everyone on the globe. Importantly, he is also beyond the reach of the Antichrist and his demons, whose activity is now restricted to the earth (12:7-9).

This preaching angel is unreachable and untouchable because the spiritual battle between angels and demons is, at this time, presumably over. He announces an "eternal gospel" containing unchangeable truths. This is the only mention in John's writings of the word *gospel* (Greek, *euangelion*).

The good news this angel delivers is that there is still time. And this is good news that we can deliver to people today as well.

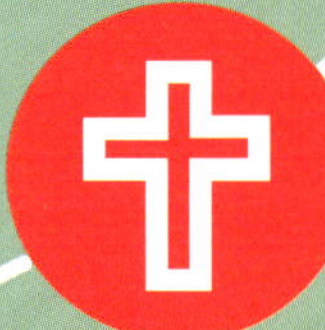

THE GOSPEL ANGEL'S GOSPEL MESSAGE

Revelation 14:7

1. **"Fear God"**—This is a warning to fear God, not the tyrannical world leader known as the "beast." Most have rejected the gospel by this time, yet God gives them one last chance to believe before accepting the mark of the beast (666), and thus, forever sealing their damnation (Revelation 14:9-11).

   The angel's message is addressed to "those who live on the earth" (verse 6), a phrase used throughout the book of Revelation that refers to the masses of unbelieving humanity. Also, it is addressed to "every nation and tribe and tongue and people" (verse 6). This signifies that the angel's message will reach the entire planet, finally fulfilling Christ's prophecy in Matthew 24:14:

   > This gospel of the kingdom shall be preached in the whole world as a testimony to all the nations, and then the end will come.

2. **"Give Him glory"**—It's time to acknowledge the God of heaven, not the "god of this world" (2 Corinthians 4:4). And why do this? "Because the hour of His *judgment* has come" (Revelation 14:7, emphasis added). The final set of Revelation's judgments are coming. Armageddon is coming. Jesus is coming!

3. **"Worship Him"**—The first and most fundamental way we understand God is by seeing Him as the Creator (Romans 1:18-22). He "who made the heaven and the earth and sea and springs of waters" (Revelation 14:7). But if people are persuaded that God is not the Creator, they will never embrace Him as Lord. Worshipping this God means submitting and surrendering to Him, which is exactly what the Antichrist will demand from people at this time through the mark of the beast (Revelation 13:12-18).

THE BAD-NEWS-BABYLON ANGEL

REVELATION 14:8

Revelation 14:8 marks the first time the word *Babylon* appears in Revelation.

Notifications

ALERT!

REVELATION 14:8

FALLEN, FALLEN IS
BABYLON THE GREAT...

Babylon is portrayed as a harlot (Revelation 17:5), which encompasses its religious nature in seducing the world's nations to become "drunk with the wine of her immorality" (verse 2). The imagery, in one of the seven bowl angel's words, is Babylon offers the world a cup of wine, making her drunk with allegiance to the Antichrist. Ironically, God will soon force the Antichrist and all those in his kingdom to drink His own cup of wine, one mixed with His fierce wrath (14:10; 16:19; 18:6).

This is why Revelation 17:5 says Babylon the great is the mother of harlots—referring to the final apostate world religion that spreads across the planet in the tribulation's beginning, and which prepares for the worship of the beast.

So, this angel announces the inevitable collapse and destruction of Babylon, which occurs at the end of the tribulation (18:10).

QUICK FACTS: BABYLON

- Mentioned six times in Revelation
- Mentioned around 300 times in Scripture
- In virtually every instance, it refers to a literal city

BABYLON IN SCRIPTURE

- Babylon is a picture of rebellion against God.
- It first appears in Genesis 10:10—it is where the kingdom of Nimrod (Noah's descendant through Ham) began.
- Babel was the first site of an idolatrous religion, as the Tower of Babel was an expression of a global rejection of God (11:5-9).
- In Babylonian, the word means "the gateway to the gods."
- In Hebrew, the word means "confusion."
- In Revelation, Babylon is both the Antichrist's government headquarters as well as the symbol of his entire kingdom.

THE *REALLY-* BAD-NEWS ANGEL

REVELATION 14:9-13

We could also call this being that will fly across midheaven the final warning angel. All told, there are six angels that appear in Revelation 14 (verses 6, 8, 9, 15, 17, 18). Specifically, this third announcing angel warns humanity that whoever takes the mark of the beast will end up in the lake of fire (verses 9-11). Taking the mark seals a person's destiny forever, and it is impossible to repent after receiving it.

The warning angel's message is clear: Receive the mark and you will drink of the wine of the wrath of God.

The angel emphasizes that God's wrath will be mixed in "full strength" (verse 10), or undiluted. Nothing is held back. It's the strongest it can possibly be. A hundred-proof wrath. Fermented fury. Accepting the Antichrist's mark is a conscious decision that carries eternal consequences (16:2; 20:4).

THE FULL-STRENGTH WRATH OF GOD

- **It is poured out in the Lamb's presence, and the angels also witness it (verse 10).** Because God is omnipresent, He is present in hell, yet relationally separated from those who are there (Matthew 27:46). The fact that He is present and witnessing their torment makes their suffering even worse. And every person who is present is there because they consciously chose to be (Revealtion 14:11).
- **It is eternal—"forever and ever" (verse 11).** It lasts for as long as God does. For ages and ages. It is unending and unceasing.
- **It is unrelenting.** This passage tells us that those under God's eternal wrath "have no rest day and night" (verse 11). Truly nothing is worse than this (see Matthew 25:46; Mark 9:48). And yet, when this third angel flies over the earth, God still—even at this late hour—offers a way out. An escape. A rescue from His retribution.

Conversely, those in the tribulation who trust in Jesus are blessed and rewarded. A voice from heaven declares, "Blessed are the dead who die in the Lord from now on!" The Spirit replies, "Yes... so that they may rest from their labors, for their deeds follow with them" (Revelation 14:13).

OTHER END-TIMES ANGELS

HARVEST AND WINEPRESS *(Revelation 14)*

- An angel prompts "one like a son of man" to harvest the earth (verses 14-16).
- An angel with a sickle (verse 17) gathers "clusters from the vine of the earth" and throws the grapes into the "great wine press of the wrath of God" (verse 19).
- An angel who has "power over fire" commands the angel with the sickle to do their reaping (verse 18).

SEVEN BOWL ANGELS *(Revelation 15)*

- They emerge from "the temple of the tabernacle of testimony in heaven" (verse 5).
- They are "clothed in linen, clean and bright" and wear golden sashes (verse 6).
- One of the four living creatures from around God's throne gives seven golden bowls "full of the wrath of God" to the bowl angels (verse 7).
- Once the bowl angels emerge, no one will be able to enter the temple until all seven plagues are finished (verse 8).

PART 5

CHOOSING YOUR FLIGHT PATH:

RESPONSES TO PROPHECY AND ESCHATOLOGY

The prophecies found in the Bible are not present for our entertainment or to simply satisfy our curiosity concerning the end times. Instead, they are there for us to believe in and to respond to. Throughout the story of Scripture, individuals have been confronted with God's proclamations about the future—from prophecies regarding Israel and the nations to ones about the coming of the promised Messiah.

But God isn't finished fulfilling His prophecies, as there are yet some 500 left that remain unfulfilled. Many of these will come to pass during the last days. But first, let's look back to see how some of those in the Bible responded to God's declarations and what we can learn from them.

ANGELS AND PROPHETS

1 PETER 1:10-12

As to this salvation, the prophets who prophesied of the grace that would come to you made careful searches and inquiries, seeking to know what person or time the Spirit of Christ within them was indicating as He predicted the sufferings of Christ and the glories to follow. It was revealed to them that they were not serving themselves, but you, in these things which now have been announced to you through those who preached the gospel to you by the Holy Spirit sent from heaven—things into which angels long to look.

The angels and prophets longed to understand the big picture of Bible prophecy.

The prophets received prophecy from God, but did not have or comprehend the full picture. This passage tells us they searched carefully, longing to understand the complete picture. Specifically, they wanted to understand who the Messiah would be, when He would arrive for His time of suffering, and were curious about the glories that would follow (i.e., the second advent and future kingdom age).

For example, the prophet Daniel asked for more understanding about the prophecies he was receiving from his heavenly messenger, but was told, "Go your way, Daniel, for these words will be kept secret and sealed up until the end time" (Daniel 12:9 NASB).

Also, notice that the angels yearn to investigate and fathom matters of prophecy and salvation. They will only ever know God as Creator. We are privileged to know Him as both Creator and Redeemer!

ABRAHAM

Abraham acted on prophecy.

Abraham responded to prophecy with his feet. Though he was from a pagan land and given no concrete information about where he was to go, Abraham's faith in God's promise (i.e., prophecy) moved him to obedient and immediate action.

The Abrahamic Promise stands as one of the key ongoing and unconditional prophecies in the Bible. He was promised a land, a people, and a worldwide blessing. That land is Israel, the people are the Jews, and the worldwide blessing is Jesus Christ—the Savior of the world.

Though the Jewish people have experienced a hardening in part (Romans 11:25), the purpose of the future tribulation period is to help them see that Jesus is indeed the Messiah and, one day, "all Israel will be saved" (Romans 11:26).

GENESIS 12:1-4

The LORD said to Abram, "Go from your country, and from your relatives and from your father's house, to the land which I will show you; and I will make you into a great nation, and I will bless you, and make your name great; and you shall be a blessing; and I will bless those who bless you, and the one who curses you I will curse. And in you all the families of the earth will be blessed." So Abram went away as the LORD had spoken to him (NASB).

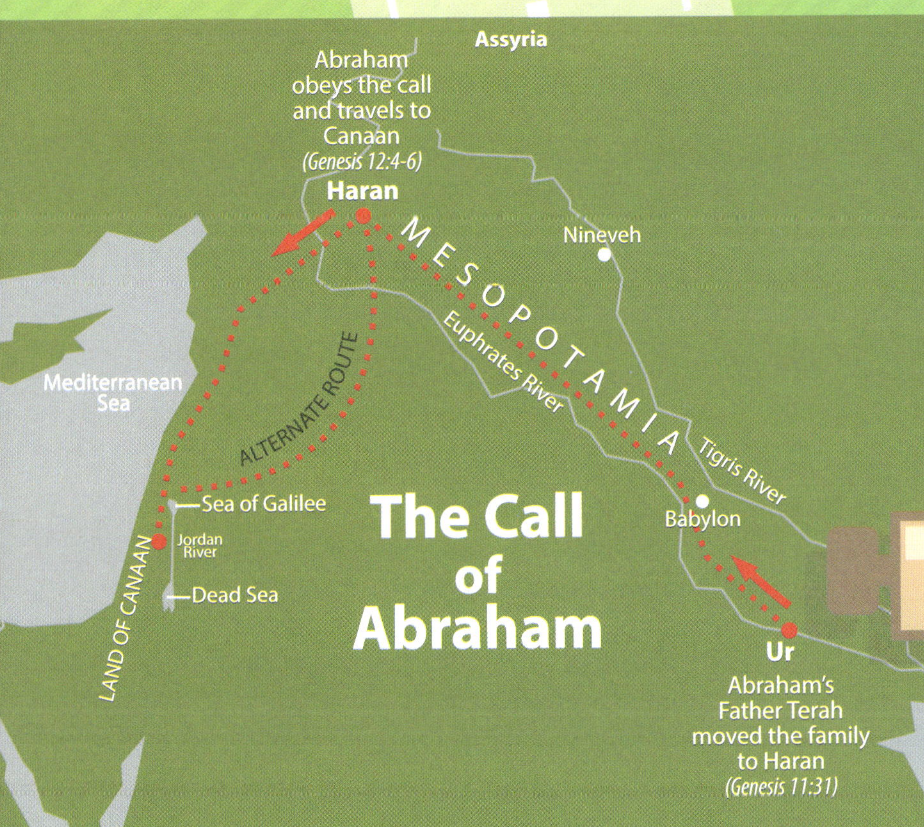

MARY

LUKE 1:30-33

The angel said to her, "Do not be afraid, Mary, for you have found favor with God. And behold, you will conceive in your womb and give birth to a son, and you shall name Him Jesus. He will be great and will be called the Son of the Most High; and the Lord God will give Him the throne of His father David; and He will reign over the house of Jacob forever, and His kingdom will have no end" (NASB).

LUKE 1:38

Mary said, "Behold, the Lord's bond-servant; may it be done to me according to your word." And the angel departed from her (NASB).

Mary trusted prophecy, even though it would cost her personally.

The angel Gabriel was sent to deliver a prophecy to Mary, one that would personally impact her in an immense way. She knew the public shame she would have to endure. She knew her legally bound groom might break off their engagement. She knew her life would never be the same. Yet Mary responded by trusting God's prophecy and submitted her will to the Lord.

PHARISEES

The Pharisees and Sadducees blinded themselves to the truths of prophecy—even when *the* Truth was right in front of them.

Of all the people that you would expect to embrace prophecy and recognize when it was being fulfilled before their eyes, it would have been the scribes and Pharisees who studied the Scriptures for a living. Yet, their traditions and personal comfort blinded them to the Truth—Jesus.

MATTHEW 16:1-4

The Pharisees and Sadducees came up, and putting Jesus to the test, they asked Him to show them a sign from heaven. But He replied to them, "When it is evening, you say, 'It will be fair weather, for the sky is red.' And in the morning, 'There will be a storm today, for the sky is red and threatening.' You know how to discern the appearance of the sky, but are you unable to discern the signs of the times? An evil and adulterous generation wants a sign; and so a sign will not be given to it, except the sign of Jonah." And He left them and went away (NASB).

DISCIPLES

LUKE 24:26-27

"Was it not necessary for the Christ to suffer these things and to enter into His glory?" Then beginning with Moses and with all the prophets, He explained to them the things concerning Himself in all the Scriptures.

In Luke 24, following Jesus' resurrection, two of Jesus' disciples were walking to a village called Emmaus. On the way, Jesus began traveling with them, but they didn't recognize Him. Jesus asked what they were discussing because they looked sad. Surprised, one said, "Are You the only one visiting Jerusalem and unaware of the things which have happened here in these days?" (verse 18). Then, they described how Jesus the Nazarene—one whom they believed was a prophet—had been delivered up to be crucified by the chief priests and the rulers of the Jewish people. The disciples' hopes had been dashed because they thought this Jesus would redeem Israel. And then, they related about the rumor of Jesus' resurrection.

Jesus, in His response, did not sympathize with them or give them any comfort. Instead, He said to them, "O foolish men and slow of heart to believe in all that the prophets have spoken!" (verse 25). In other words, Christ rebuked them harshly for not knowing and believing in Bible prophecy and how it related to their times. He expected them to know it and understand it, in the same way He expects His disciples today to do so as well. Then, the Lord gave them a complete survey of Bible prophecy throughout the entire Old Testament! (verses 26-27).

Today, some consider Bible prophecy to be irrelevant or unimportant. However, Jesus wants all those who claim to be His disciples to know what the prophets say about the last days and His second coming, just as He expected His disciples to know about His first coming.

JOHN

In Revelation 1, the apostle John is given an amazing vision of Jesus. This one is a much different portrayal than is in the Gospels. No longer is He walking around healing people and placing children in His lap. No, this is a Christ with whom most Christians are unfamiliar.

John's response upon seeing this Jesus was not to hug Him, but rather, be in awe of Him: "When I saw Him, I fell at His feet like a dead man" (verse 17).

The Jesus of Revelation is a glorified and exalted Christ—the One who will make Revelation's prophecies come true. Sometimes, we can be flippant toward God and forget that He is holy and worthy of our worship. John's experience here illustrates that truth. Only after responding in awe to Jesus, does the Lord reveal the reality and meaning of Revelation's prophecies to John.

REVELATION 1:13-16

In the middle of the lampstands I saw one like a son of man, clothed in a robe reaching to the feet, and girded across His chest with a golden sash. His head and His hair were white like white wool, like snow; and His eyes were like a flame of fire. His feet were like burnished bronze, when it has been made to glow in a furnace, and His voice was like the sound of many waters. In His right hand He held seven stars, and out of His mouth came a sharp two-edged sword; and His face was like the sun shining in its strength.

YOU

Like the rest of Scripture, Bible prophecy demands a response from the individual. And when it comes to Revelation and the end times, there is no shortage of erroneous reactions, ignorance, misinformation, and unbiblical conclusions.

SIX BIG MISTAKES PEOPLE MAKE WITH BIBLE PROPHECY

How Not to Respond

1 ***Manipulate It***—Some authors, teachers, and pastors sensationalize prophecy, making unfounded predictions and even committing the error of "date-setting"—a practice clearly prohibited by Scripture (Matthew 24:36). They make Scripture say more than it actually says, see a prophecy in every news headline, and their predictions never come to pass. This not only turns people off toward Bible prophecy but also discredits those who are accurately and responsibly handling it (Matthew 24:4-5, 11, 23-24; 2 Thessalonians 2:2).

2 ***Mock It***—Today, many in secular culture—and within the church—laugh at, belittle, and even mock what God says in His Word concerning the last days. But whenever this happens, they are also fulfilling Peter's prophecy found in 2 Peter 3:3-13.

3 ***Minimize or Marginalize It***—One of Satan's greatest strategies is to distract or downplay what the Bible says, even when it's obvious and staring them in the face. Many pastors don't teach the prophetic Scriptures regarding the last days. Once a year they may touch on the "Christmas prophecies" regarding Jesus' first coming, but choose to ignore the ones about the rapture or His second coming. They become like the Jewish religious leaders in Jesus' day, who dismissed the fulfillment of the Messianic prophecies, even when the One who fulfilled them was standing right in front of them! (Matthew 16:1-3; 1 Chronicles 12:32).

4 ***Miss It Altogether***—Jesus told the two disciples on the road to Emmaus that they were "foolish and slow of heart" regarding what the prophets said about Him (Luke 24:25). According to Christ, they should have studied the Scriptures enough to put the prophetic puzzle pieces together. This is the same mistake many Christians are making today. And yet, God expects us to know, believe, and anticipate their fulfillment.

5 ***Misinterpret It***—Some understand the correct interpretation of a prophecy but misconstrue the timing or application of its fulfillment. They draw incorrect conclusions concerning the meaning of the prophecy. This leads to "soft date-setting," like some who insist the rapture of the church must take place at the Jewish Feast of Trumpets. What these often well-meaning believers miss is that the rapture is exclusively a "bride event," and has nothing to do with Israel or Old Testament feasts or holidays. In their misinterpretation of the timing of Bible prophecy, they confuse Braxton-Hicks contractions to the actual biblical birth pangs (Matthew 24:8; 2 Thessalonians 2:3).

6 ***Misapply It***—When we fail to see the big picture and the totality of God's prophetic narrative, we can easily respond with fear or fatalism instead of faith and comfort. But as the Prophecy Pros often say, "Bible prophecy never produces fear. It only builds our faith!" (see Acts 1:6; 1 Thessalonians 4:18; 5:11; 2 Thessalonians 2:2; Hebrews 10:23-25).

HOW SHOULD WE RESPOND?

1 ***Believe It***—God's Word was meant to be believed because it's true. Again, we are not meant to fear or ignore Revelation, prophecy, or the future, but rather, we're meant to know it, understand and believe it, and live our lives in light of it. When studied in its proper context, prophecy always produces more faith, *not* fear.

2 ***Trust in It***—Let the Bible be your instrument panel, guiding you in your life journey.

3 ***Stand Up for It***—In a culture that mocks and misinterprets the Bible, you and I must defend it (Jude 3).

4 ***Proclaim It***—Bible prophecy is comforting, good news of hope for believers, but contains warnings and a call to salvation for unbelievers. It's up to us to do what we can to reach both groups!

PART 6

PILOT TRAINING:

PRACTICAL TIPS FOR LEADERS

Now that you have been along for the ride on this jet tour over prophecy's topography, perhaps you'd like to come up into the cockpit for a while. Maybe you're one of those people that are not merely content to know truth, but you must share it with others. If so, then this final section is important reading for you. God may be calling you to help lead others on their own prophetic journeys, sharing from Scripture what the Lord says about His last-days narrative. There are many reasons to teach Bible prophecy. Following are some encouragements and some practical reasons to incorporate sharing Bible prophecy in your ministry to others. We encourage you to explore these more deeply, and then to take your study of Bible prophecy, and your ministry through it, to the next level. Welcome to the pilot's seat.

I. WRESTLE WITH YOUR VIEW

When it comes to the various views of eschatology, we have heard many Bible teachers say things such as, "I read the end of the Bible and we win;" or, "I'm a pan-millennialist—I believe it will all pan out in the end." We don't approach other doctrines this way, and rightfully so. A studied and accurate understanding of the end helps believers live with joy, hope, courage, and purposeful urgency today. Every Bible teacher should study this important topic until they have confident convictions of their own.

II. FIND A FEW TRUSTED VOICES

We need trusted voices, other theologians who have done the hard work and packaged it for use in commentaries, books, digital media, and other resources. In a world of a million channels, anyone can develop a platform and share their opinions. It is more important than ever to vet the voices you trust—to check their qualifications, experience, point of view, and theology.

We need trusted voices who believe that all Scripture is inspired by God (2 Timothy 3:16; 1 Peter 1:20-21), inerrant, sufficient, authoritative, and complete. They need to use a literal, contextual, verbal, and plenary hermeneutic; point you deeper into God's Word; and must do so with humility and a deep love for Scripture.

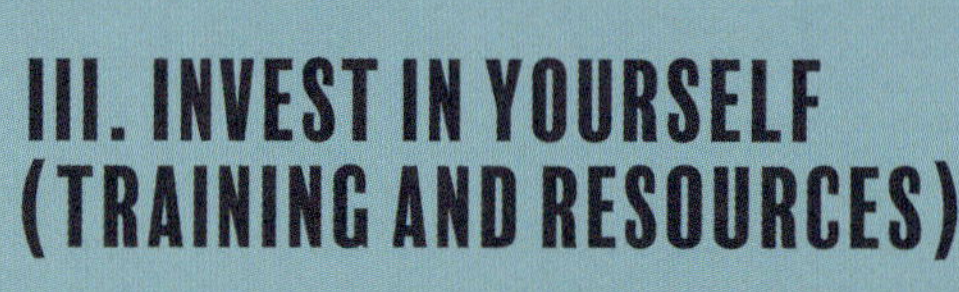

III. INVEST IN YOURSELF (TRAINING AND RESOURCES)

1 TIMOTHY 4:13-16
2 TIMOTHY 2:15

If a pastor or teacher (including yourself) needs more training, there are free online courses, paid audit courses, or (if resources allow) accredited Bible-college or seminary courses to work toward a certificate or degree. This could be the next step in their (or your) discipleship and will greatly benefit those whom they teach.

THE PILOT'S DIRECTIVE

The Bible is the only "religious" founding book that claims to be the very Word of God and backs up this claim with fulfilled prophecy. As we've detailed in this book, prophecy makes up roughly one-fourth of the Bible, is found in nearly every book of the Bible, and is tied to every key theological topic.

Both professional and lay leaders have the responsibility of presenting complete and accurate truth from God's Word. Here are five encouragements as you attempt to be faithful to your ministry calling.

IV. BRING IN SPECIALISTS

Often, pastors are quite busy with their daily demands, making it difficult to focus on a particular area of theology. To offer a body of believers a deeper level of teaching on a particular topic, good pastors will often call in specialists to teach. Many churches hold marriage conferences, financial-principles seminars, or Bible prophecy events and bring in trained specialists who have a particular calling.

V. PREACH BOLDLY

We need pastors and teachers who will declare the whole counsel of God (Acts 20:27). Preach the Word from the foundational truths of Genesis to the promised future of Revelation. The purpose of the church is to equip believers and send them out to the world, not water down the teaching and hope the world will come in. Fear God, not man. His Word is supernaturally transformative.

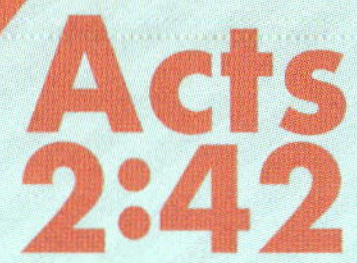

Ephesians 4:14

2 TIMOTHY 3:16-17

FLIGHT CHECKLIST: TEN REASONS TO START TEACHING BIBLE PROPHECY

I. IT'S PART OF GOD'S WORD

Because prophecy makes up nearly 30 percent of the Bible, it makes sense to study it and to know it well. All Scripture is inspired by God (2 Timothy 3:16) and Jesus told His followers to make disciples and to teach them all that He had commanded them (Matthew 28:18-20). That certainly includes His prophecies concerning the last days (Matthew 24–25; John 14:1-3).

II. IT'S A POWERFUL APOLOGETIC

Few things are more convincing than Bible prophecy. The reason for this is because it validates and authenticates the veracity and trustworthiness of the Bible. When we see that God has fulfilled all past prophecies exactly and literally as prophesied, then we can have confidence in sharing it with others to help convince them that the Bible is much more than simply an old book. In fact, it is the living Word of God and it can change their lives (Hebrews 4:12).

III. IT'S AN AUTOMATIC DISCIPLE GENERATOR

To be a disciple means to be a learner. As a follower of Christ, you never want to stop learning. Instead, you want to grow in the grace and knowledge of Jesus and of His Word. Since prophecy is largely neglected by many pastors and most Christians, part of your discipleship is discovering what God has to say not only about the future of the world, but also about your future as well. Bible prophecy will give you that information. It's like sitting at the feet of Jesus, just as the disciples did on the Mount of Olives in Matthew 24. The more you study Bible prophecy and understand it properly, the stronger your faith will be.

IV. IT PROVIDES A FRAMEWORK FOR DISCERNMENT

When Paul wrote to the Thessalonians, they were very confused and upset about the end times and the last days. This is because there had been a lot of misinformation spread by some false teachers that had crept in to the church (2 Thessalonians 2:1-2). Paul's antidote to this deception and confusion was to teach them about Bible prophecy again. In fact, Paul was very specific about the chronology of God's end-times events, even to the point of describing what the Antichrist would do and when the rapture would occur in relationship to Him (verses 3-9). The more you study God's Word and Bible prophecy, the more wisdom and discernment you will have concerning the world, humanity, and the future.

V. IT GIVES CLARITY AND CONFIDENCE FOR TODAY

This discernment essentially allows you to "see in the dark." Because you know prophecy, it gives you a great sense of confidence to stand boldly for God's truth in this world. It eliminates your fear of the future or of the present, because you know Who oversees all these things. It has been said that knowledge is power, and that is true, especially in an age of ignorance and lies. But knowledge also imparts light, and light in a dark world inspires great confidence. You can be sure of what you believe, even when many around you will doubt and deny your beliefs and what Scripture says.

VI. IT GIVES HOPE FOR TOMORROW

Paul concluded his teaching on the rapture in 1 Thessalonians 4 by stating, "Therefore comfort one another with these words" (verse 18). The promise of the future that Jesus has planned for us gives us nothing but comfort and hope. Keep in mind that in the Bible, the word *hope* does not mean "wishing something." Instead, it means to confidently expect something. And we know that Jesus is in heaven right now preparing a place for us, and that all who place their trust in Jesus have a bright and hopeful future (John 14:1-3).

FLIGHT CHECKLIST: TEN REASONS TO START TEACHING BIBLE PROPHECY

VII. IT INSPIRES URGENCY

Christians should never panic, because they know that God is in charge. However, there should be a sense of purposeful urgency about our lives. This is because we are living in the last days and our life on this earth is relatively short. We must heed Paul's instructions to the Ephesians, when he said, "Be careful how you walk...making the most of your time, because the days are evil" (Ephesians 5:15-16).

Our purpose is to glorify God and our mandate is to make disciples. And we have no time to waste. Whatever you are going to do for God, you must do it now. This is your time. This is your moment!

VIII. IT IMPARTS BLESSING

The book of Revelation is the only book in the Bible that promises a blessing if you read it, hear it, and obey it (Revelation 1:3). Part of the blessing of Revelation is that you get to know what is going to happen in the future, so that you can warn others to avoid the judgment that takes place in chapters 6–19. Another blessing of Revelation is that you get to know God better. In fact, as we have seen, His attributes are on open display throughout the entire book. A result of studying prophecy is that you grow closer to Jesus and love Him more. Revelation 19:10 says, "The testimony of Jesus is the spirit of prophecy." So if you study Bible prophecy, and do it properly, you will find yourself more in love with Jesus Christ. And what could be a greater blessing than that?

IX. IT STRENGTHENS PERSEVERANCE

To all the churches in Revelation 2–3, Jesus promised a very special blessing to "who overcomes" (Revelation 2:7, 11, 17, 26; 3:5, 12, 21). In fact, every true believer is an overcomer (Romans 8:37; 1 John 4:4). Knowing that we win in the end helps us to persevere in the present. And Hebrews 10:25 tells us to greatly encourage one another here in these last days. We need one another as we walk through these dark times together. And when we see our brethren walking in strength and continuing on day by day, it encourages us to do the same, to run the race well, and to finish strong (1 Corinthians 9:24-27).

X. IT ORDERS PRIORITIES

Imagine if your house was on fire. What would you grab and save other than your family? This illustration tells you something of what's really important to you. It shows you what your priorities are. Priorities are motivated by our passions. And our passions are fueled by our faith. Once we study Bible prophecy, we discover what is really important to God in these last days. We discover what His priorities are. That helps us take a good look at our own lives and to make sure that God is number 1, our families are number 2, and our ministries are number 3. If we have these priorities in order, then everything else will naturally fall into place. The apostle John, under the inspiration of the Holy Spirit, wrote concerning the rapture return of Jesus:

> Beloved, now we are children of God, and it has not appeared as yet what we will be. We know that when He appears, we will be like Him, because we will see Him just as He is. And everyone who has this hope fixed on Him purifies himself, just as He is pure (1 John 3:2-3).

It is our prayer that this book has done more than simply inform you, but that God's Word has transformed you. We hope that you sense a renewed intimacy with our Lord and that you are inspired to press on with boldness, strength, and confidence in these perilous last days!

NOTES

1. American Bible Society and Barna Group, "State of the Bible 2021: Five Key Findings," *Barna* (May 19, 2021), at https://www.barna.com/research/sotb-2021/.
2. The context of this chapter and its prophecies, beginning in verse 24, along with biblical history, make it clear that Daniel's "weeks" are periods of seven years. Therefore "seventy weeks" corresponds to 70 x 7 = 490 years. Four hundred and eighty-three (seven weeks and 62 weeks) of those years is described as the time period from the "issuing of a decree to restore and rebuild Jerusalem until Messiah the Prince" (Daniel 9:25). Then, following the 62 weeks, "the Messiah will be cut off" (verse 26). This amazing prophecy was fulfilled to the day! This is followed by a "prophetic gap" between the sixty-ninth and seventieth weeks. That last week (of seven years) is the time described covering the Antichrist's treaty with Israel.
3. Maayan Jaffe-Hoffman, "Number of Jews in Israel and Worldwide on the Rise," *The Jerusalem Post* (September 27, 2019), at https://www.jpost.com/israel-news/number-of-jews-in-israel-and-worldwide-on-the-rise-reports-603033.
4. Calculations taken from *The Revelation Record* by Dr. Henry Morris (Carol Stream, IL: Tyndale, 1983), 450-451.
5. Satan's fall must have occurred at some point after creation but before the fall. Scripture says he was with God at the time of creation, and he next appears in the garden of Eden.
6. See 1 John 2:18, 22; 4:3; 2 John 7.
7. The Bible never records that righteous angels are ever bound as these four are.
8. Combine the numbers from Revelation 6:8 with 9:15.
9. See Genesis 19:24, 28, where fire and brimstone are used in judgment.
10. See Deuteronomy 32:17; Psalm 106:36-37; 1 Corinthians 10:20-21.
11. Robert Thomas, *Revelation 8–22: An Exegetical Commentary* (Chicago: Moody Publishers, 1995), 54.
12. See also Galatians 5:20; Revelation 18:23; 21:8; 22:15.
13. Genesis 6:1-2; 19:1ff. For more on how Noah's world parallels our own, see Jeff Kinley, *As It Was in the Days of Noah* (Eugene, OR: Harvest House Publishers, 2014).

ALSO BY THE PROPHECY PROS

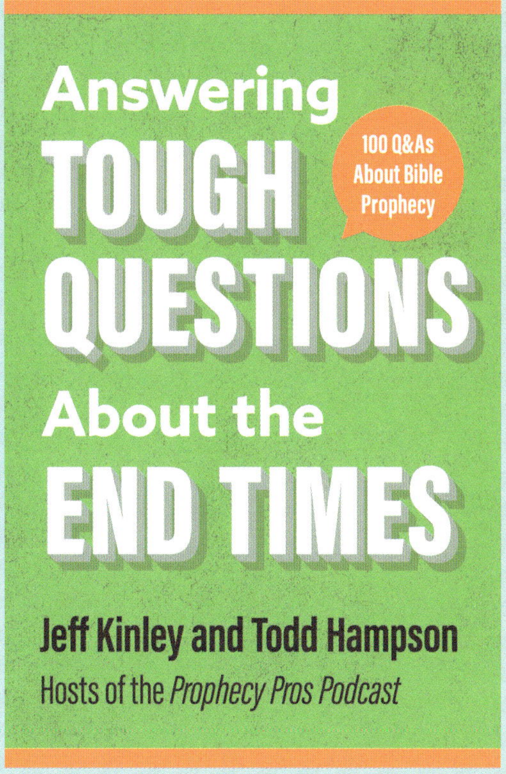

In a field often clouded by complexity and sensationalism, keeping track of what the Bible says about the end times can be challenging even for seasoned believers. That's why the bestselling authors behind the *Prophecy Pros Podcast* are here to bring you a comprehensive and user-friendly guide to the most need-to-know facts about what is to come.

Neatly organized and packed with charts, timelines, and infographics, *Answering Tough Questions About the End Times* delivers clear answers to 100 of the most pressing questions about the last days. As you learn about what Bible prophecy is and where it's found in Scripture, you will also find speculation-free and biblically sourced overviews of forthcoming events such as the rapture, Jesus' second coming, and life in heaven.

As you grow in your understanding of God's plans for history still-to-come, your trust in Him will be transformed. Whether you're new to your faith or a longtime student of Bible prophecy, this approachable handbook will provide helpful, straightforward answers to your queries and concerns about the end times, inspiring you to face the future with confidence!

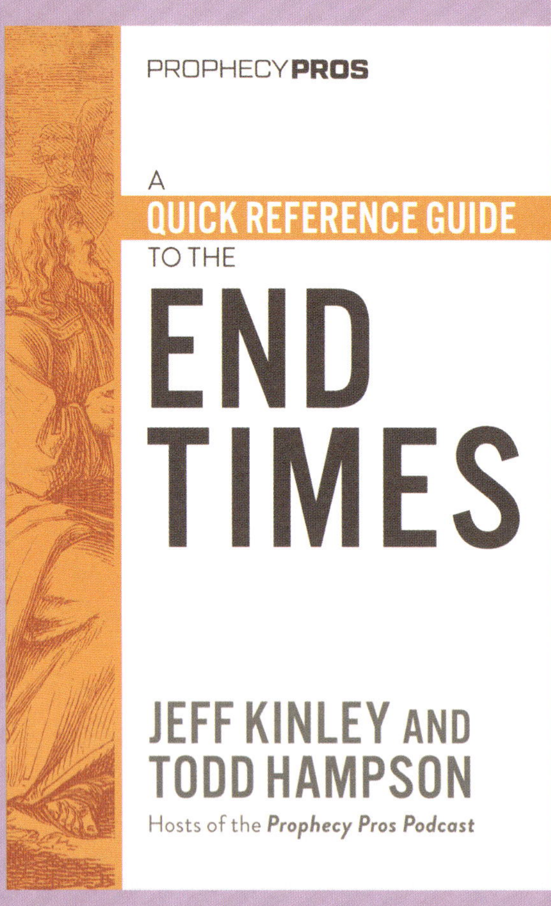

From the team behind the *Prophecy Pros Podcast* comes *A Quick Reference Guide to the End Times*—a concise look at the most pressing questions about the rapture, the Antichrist, the millennial kingdom, and beyond. Jeff and Todd share their wealth of Scripture-based knowledge about the end times, steering away from speculation to make sure you get only the information that truly matters.

Featuring helpful charts, graphics, and illustrations, this accessible manual will help you understand answers to important prophecy questions such as...

- in what basic order will the end times unfold?
- how do we know Jesus is literally returning to earth?
- how should Christians live if Jesus might return any day now?

Whether you're totally new to Bible prophecy or you've been studying it for years, *A Quick Reference Guide to the End Times* is the user-friendly handbook you need to keep track of the most essential facts about the future.

OTHER GREAT HARVEST HOUSE RESOURCES

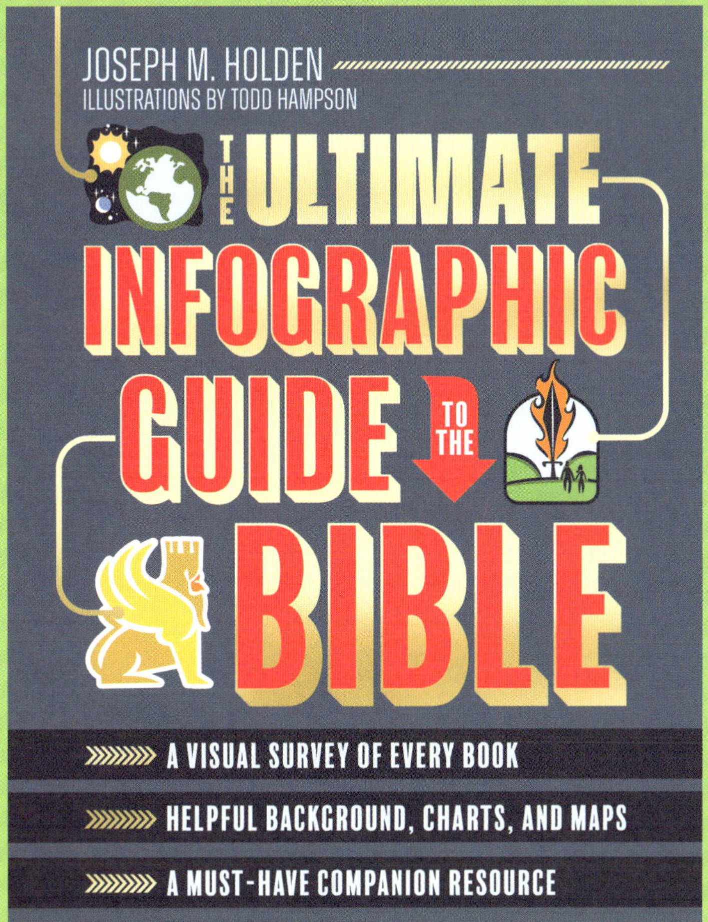

A BIRD'S-EYE VIEW OF THE BIBLE

Whether you're reading God's Word for the first time or the fortieth, you're bound to ask questions along the way: *Why can I be confident the Bible is reliable? Who decided which books made the final cut? What else do I need to know to get the most out of what I'm reading?*

For new and seasoned believers alike, *The Ultimate Infographic Guide to the Bible* delivers invaluable historical, cultural, and contextual insights so you can better understand Scripture. These fascinating charts, graphics, and timelines will enrich your reading experience by

- highlighting the key events, themes, and applications found in each book of the Bible
- providing background on the Bible's reliability, translation process, and preservation
- illuminating how God's strength, power, and love are revealed throughout the Bible's overarching story

The Ultimate Infographic Guide to the Bible will equip you to understand the significance of every part of the Bible—and witness how each incredible truth God makes known to His people is relevant to you today.

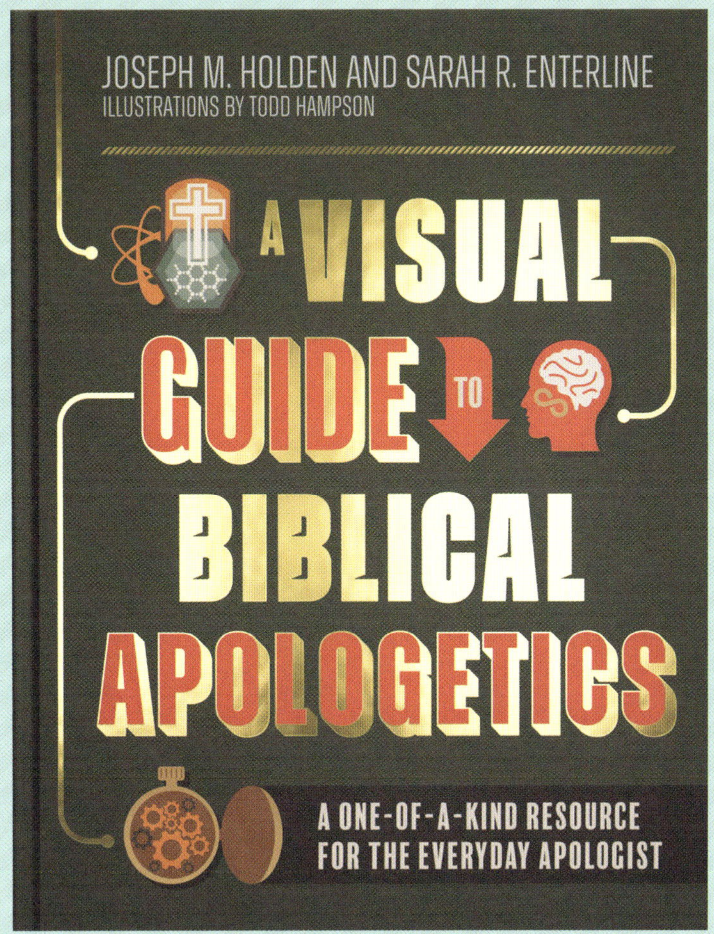

SHARING YOUR FAITH JUST GOT EASIER

The intersection of Christianity and secular culture is commonly filled with disagreement, tension, and complicated issues, leading many Christians to avoid talking about their faith entirely. But when we discover the astounding ways Christianity is both true and transformative—the goal of apologetics—everything changes!

Clear, concise, and easy to use, this introductory guide to apologetics takes the fear out of sharing your faith and biblical truth. As a *visual* guide, this one-of-a-kind resource features engaging infographics, charts, and tables that make difficult concepts a breeze to understand. You will find accessible explanations about all the major apologetics topics, including

- the existence of God
- the problem of evil
- faith versus reason
- Christianity and the major world religions
- the trustworthiness of the Bible
- evolution and science
- Jesus and salvation
- moral relativism versus absolute truth
- and more!

Regardless of your age, background, or learning style, *A Visual Guide to Biblical Apologetics* will equip you to address many issues with clarity and conviction. As your confidence in the good reasons for belief grows, you won't be able to help but share them with those around you!

PAL
PROPHECY AIRLINES

Time to fly!

Time to fly!

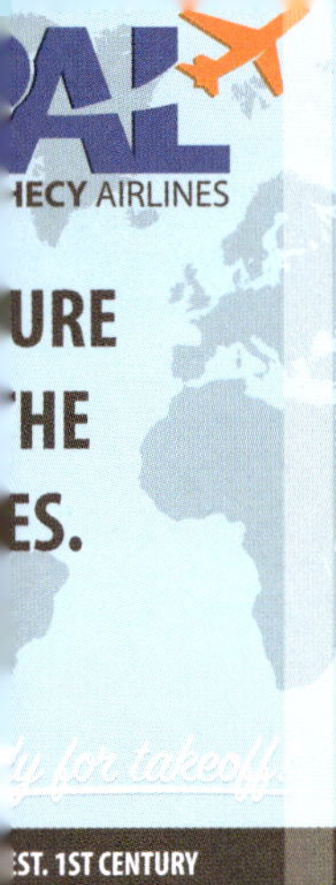

Time to fly!

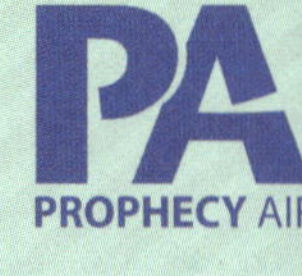

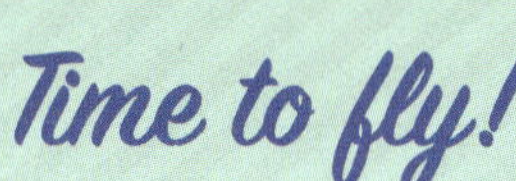